CIVIL WAR
Women

Their Quilts • Their Roles • Activities for Re-Enactors

Barbara Brackman

C&T PUBLISHING

©2000 Barbara Brackman
Illustrations ©2000 C&T Publishing, Inc.

Editor: Liz Aneloski
Technical Editor: Sara Kate MacFarland
Copy Editor: Steven Cook
Cover and Book Designer/Design Director: Kristen Yenche
Production Coordination: Diane Pedersen
Production Assistant: Kirstie L. McCormick
Illustrator: Alan McCorkle
Photographer: Jon Blumb, unless otherwise noted
Author Photo: John Gary Brown
Front Cover: *Seven Sisters* (detail) by Cherie Ralston, Back Cover: *Tobacco Worm* by Cherie Ralston
Published by C&T Publishing, Inc., P.O. Box 1456, Lafayette, California 94549

Attention Teachers:
C&T Publishing, Inc. encourages you to use this book as a text for teaching. Contact us at 800-284-1114 or www.ctpub.com for more information about the C&T Teachers Program.

We take great care to ensure that the information included in this book is accurate and presented in good faith, but no warranty is provided nor results guaranteed. Since we have no control over the choice of materials or procedures used, neither the author nor C&T Publishing, Inc. shall have any liability to any person or entity with respect to any loss or damage caused directly or indirectly by the information contained in this book.

Trademarked (™) and Registered Trademarked (®) names are used throughout this book. Rather than use the symbols with every occurrence of a trademark and registered trademark name, we are using the names only in an editorial fashion and to the benefit of the owner, with no intention of infringement.

Library of Congress Cataloging-in-Publication Data

Brackman, Barbara.
  Civil War women : their quilts, their roles, activities for
re-enactors / Barbara Brackman.
      p. cm.
    ISBN 1-57120-104-1
1. United States—History—Civil War, 1861-1865—Women. 2.
United States—History—Civil War, 1861-1865—Social aspects. 3.
Women—United States—Biography. 4. Women—United States—Social
conditions—19th century. 5. Women—United States—Social life
and customs—19th century. 6. Historical reenactments—United
States. 7. Quilts—United States—History—19th century. 8.
Quilting—Handbooks, manuals, etc. I. Title.
    E628 .B83 2000
    973.7'082—dc21

                                              00-008239

Printed in Hong Kong
10 9 8 7 6 5 4 3 2 1

CONTENTS

Introduction

"Tis very pleasant to write one's thoughts sometimes. Though paltry and insignificant to another, to you they posess (sic) a value that can be known by none other than yourself. A thought then unexpressed would pass from the mind, and with it the whole train that accompanied it, once put in words will whenever read bring back it's (sic) companions. They are the keepers of those bright fancies and struggles of spirit, that refuse to be caged in words." October 7, 1861, Grace Brown Elmore.

Two women pose before a field station of the U.S. Sanitary Commission in Virginia in 1863. The Sanitary Commission, the precursor of today's Red Cross, was a welcome presence wherever the Union Army traveled.

This is my second book about quilts and America's Civil War. In the first, *Quilts from the Civil War,* I took a broad view, exploring average women's roles during the War and how they used quilts as fundraisers and vehicles for patriotic and political expression and to aid soldiers. This second book revisits the subject for an in-depth view of women's individual lives. In each of the nine stories, we see the effects of the War on women's lives in Victorian society.

Some women played out their traditional roles, supporting men as mothers, wives, and sweethearts. Others, like nurse Hannah Ropes and seamstress Rachel Cormany, supported themselves and the cause by working outside their homes in jobs restricted to women. Newspaper correspondent Julia Lovejoy, lecturer Lucy Stone, and government clerk Cornelia Colton took on unusual roles, out in the world of men. And too many women played the parts thrust upon them. Bursheba Younger was a refugee, Dolly Lunt Burge a widow managing a plantation, and Susie Taylor King an emancipated slave.

Most of the women's stories are drawn from women's writings, their diaries, letters, and memoirs. In their written words, I have left the grammar and spelling errors as they appeared in print, but with spoken words transcribed by someone else into dialect I have paraphrased the dialect into regular English, making the words more immediate. To encourage the reader to continue reading these stories, I've included lists for further reading about women living similar lives. Nothing makes those times more tangible than women's day-by-day accounts.

Again, as in my previous book, I encourage the reader to forge a personal link to the women of the Civil War era by copying the quilts of the day. Each woman is matched to a quilt; one that I imagine she might have made. Some designs bear obvious war messages in their patriotic or militaristic motifs; other patterns have symbolic meaning, a message hidden in the name or design.

For the many who enjoy re-enacting Civil War women's lives, I have offered activities for re-enactors, relating each woman's role to personal interpretations. The stories offer a view of camp life beyond the usual activities like laundry and cooking. More challenging jobs, such as newspaper correspondents, smugglers, or lecturers, were available at the time. The reading lists on pages 120-122 will add to your interpretation.

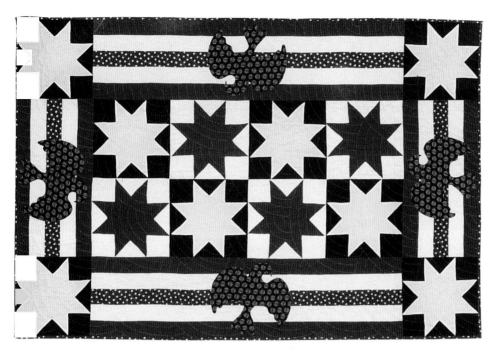

UNION STAR, hand appliquéd, machine pieced, and hand quilted by Bobbi Finley, San Jose, California, 1998, 48" x 72". Quilts and the Civil War are two elements which shape American myth and the ways we view our past. Sometimes myth stretches beyond history. Quilt patterns and their names symbolize different meanings to different generations. Bobbi's quilt is a copy of a reproduction sold as an authentic souvenir of Lincoln's second election. Reproduction quilts should be enjoyed as links to the past, but collectors must be careful in their purchases and historians cautious in their conclusions.

The quilt patterns offer handwork for the re-enactor who knows that no respectable lady of the 1860s would sit with idle hands. Patchwork, then as now, offers a creative and pleasant way to pass the time.

In this book, as in the last, I've relied on my circle of friends for help with quilts, patterns, and designs. I want to thank Jon Blumb for his photography, and, for their models and friendship, the women I sew with on Thursdays: Terry Thompson, Jean Stanclift, Cherie Ralston, Karla Menaugh, Pam Mayfield, and Shauna Christensen. And many thanks to other more far-flung friends and quiltmakers: Judy Davis, Barbara Eikmeier, Bobbi Finley, Linda Frost, Janet Finley, Mary Fischer-Boyd, Nancy Hornback, Lori Isenberger, Mary Madden, Rosie Mayhew, Mary Ellen Nichols, Nancy Wakefield, and Jeananne Wright. I also want to thank Erma Kirkpatrick, Carol Smith, and Terry Thompson for loaning quilts for photography.

CHAPTER 1

REMEMBERING LUCY STONE AND OTHER WOMEN LECTURERS

"Miss Angelina Grimké exhibited considerable talent for a female as an orator; appeared not at all abashed in exhibiting herself in a position so unsuitable to her sex, totally disregarding the doctrine of St. Paul, who says 'Is it not a shame of a woman to speak in public?' She belabored the slaveholders and beat the air like all possessed."[1]

The eagle, symbolizing the United States, clutches both arrows and olive branches—the threat of war and the hope of peace. A dozen or so nineteenth-century eagle quilts with the bird carrying a banner blazing "liberty" and talons holding only arrows, survive. This warrior eagle, with his demand for liberty for all, seems to promise no quarter, give no hope for compromise or peace. Such a strident voice reflects the message of abolitionists like Abby Kelley, Angelina Grimké, and Lucy Stone in the years before the Civil War.

Lucy Stone (1818-1893) carried liberty's banner from 1847 until long after the War's end. A feminist as well as an abolitionist, she was born in Massachusetts in 1818, the eighth of nine children. Bright and hungry for an education, she later recalled "a time when I needed a school book which father thought a *girl* need not have, and I went with my little bare toes and gathered chestnuts enough to buy one, and then felt a prouder triumph than I have known ever since."[2] When her father refused to educate her as he had her brothers, she resolved to earn her tuition, not by gathering chestnuts but through traditional women's work, teaching and housekeeping. When she was 29, she graduated from the Oberlin Collegiate Institute in Ohio, one of the few colleges to give degrees to women. Her father had grown to realize her determination and loaned her money for her final year. After teaching for a year to earn enough money to repay him, Lucy embarked on the lecture circuit.

Oberlin was a hotbed of radicalism where anti-slavery ideas were part of the curriculum. Graduates joined a fraternity of free-thinkers to which women were welcome. Among them, Lucy could answer her calling to lecture despite the fact that "women speakers," as Julia Ward Howe said, "were few in those days, and were frowned upon by general society."[3]

Women compelled to speak might begin with a "parlour talk" limited to women. Howe recalled her first "parlour lectures," where she "commissioned certain of my friends to invite certain of their friends to my house for an appointed evening."[4]

Opposite page
WORDS WERE THE ABOLITIONISTS' most important weapon. Antique blocks feature inked signatures and sentiments from the 1850s, the years when Lucy Stone's words shaped anti-slavery thought. Linda Frost's 1998 quilt reflects Stone's ideals—the ideals of the nation's founder, Washington, revered by patriots in both the Union and the Confederacy. The charcoal drawing depicts Washington's tomb at Mount Vernon overlooking the Potomac.

Several women speakers, Lucy among them, outgrew the parlors and learned how to fill churches and halls. She knew the lesson that Thomas Wentworth Higginson, a fellow lecturer on the abolitionist circuit, thought most important to becoming a presence on the platform. "Enlist in a reform. Engage in something which you feel for the moment to be so unspeakably more important than yourself as wholly to dwarf you." Higginson remembered well other women on the anti-slavery speaking circuits of the 1840s and '50s. "My own teachers were the slave women who came shyly before the audience. . . . women who had been stripped and whipped and handled with insolent hands and sold to the highest bidder. . . . We learned to speak because their presence made silence impossible. . . . I cannot remember one really poor speaker. As [Ralph Waldo] Emerson said 'eloquence was dog-cheap there.' "[5]

Realizing their effectiveness, abolition organizations paid speakers to travel and awaken Americans to the injustices of slavery. In 1848, Lucy became a salaried agent for the Massachusetts Anti-Slavery Society. Carefully balancing her speechmaking, she did their bidding on weekends and spoke about women's rights during the week, explaining, "I was a woman before I was an abolitionist." She became such a draw that when she charged a small admission she earned $7,000 in three years. Her reputation rose above the mere novelty of a lady lecturer. "Lucy is Queen of us all," wrote Higginson, "and delights the whole country from Maine to Kentucky. . . . You have no idea of [her] eloquence and power."[6]

WARRIOR EAGLE, machine pieced and hand appliquéd by Janet Finley, Arvada, Colorado, 1999, 58" x 58". Hand and machine quilted. The stuffed stars were quilted by machine. Janet made her quilt in memory of Alfred Lees, her husband's relative who died of wounds received at the Battle of Gettysburg in July, 1863, when he was 19 years old.

On the road in Cincinnati, Lucy met a like-minded younger man, Henry Blackwell, "a short, stout, pleasant-looking person, with very black hair and whiskers, blue eyes and a good forehead."[7] Born of a liberal family, Blackwell had a sister Elizabeth, who was the first woman doctor to graduate from an American medical institution.[8] Long before she met Henry, Lucy had vowed never to marry. Memories of an overbearing father and a meek mother colored her view of a marriage contract that declared women the lesser partner legally, economically, intellectually, and emotionally. But Henry wooed her relentlessly, promising a different kind of marriage—a union of equals.

Henry may have been her soulmate, but he had little understanding of the role of flattery in courtship. "[A friend] says you are not beautiful. To me your person is perfectly lovely. When I first knew you I used sometimes to wish you had a prettier nose, I remember. But now, I would not have your nose altered for the world."[9] To our view, Lucy is attractive, with rather broad features, expressive lips, and eyes that must have flashed with passion that reached from the lecture platform to the back of the hall.

When Henry Blackwell met Lucy she wore reform dress. He wrote his brother of his affection for her, "I decidedly prefer her to any lady I have ever met, always excepting the Bloomer dress which I *don't* like practically, tho theoretically I believe in it with my whole soul." He later wrote Lucy after visiting Angelina and Sarah Grimké, "We first met the two ladies draped in the Bloomer costume, which I have learned to like of late."[10]

Lucy wore reform dress for several years, but decided the sensationalism detracted from her message. By the 1860s, bloomers had evolved. The pants were straight-legged, without the elastic that looked like Turkish costume, and the short dress was much like other Civil-War era dress: round necked, waistline at the waist, with full sleeves, but certainly *no* hoops.

After much consideration, captured in their correspondence, Lucy agreed to marry Henry Blackwell. In his journal, their close friend Higginson described the wedding he conducted. "In came the small lady and with her the bridegroom; he in the proper white waistcoat, she in a beautiful silk ashes-of-roses color. They stood up together and they read their protest. . . . She had some scruples about the form, but seemed to think a great deal of what her mother would wish. . . . so she expressed her purpose to 'love and honor' (not obey) very clearly and sweetly."[11]

From "Peterson's Magazine," 1851
The exceptional bloomers

REFORM DRESS "Bloomer Costume" as pictured in *Peterson's Magazine* in 1851, the year Elizabeth Smith Miller appeared in public in "Turkish Trousers." The outfit was soon copied by other feminists such as Elizabeth Cady Stanton and Amelia Jenks Bloomer, who created a national sensation by advocating reform dress in her newspaper *The Lily.*

Lucy's protest against conventional marriage included a wish to use her maiden name. As Lucy Stone and Henry Blackwell, the couple worked hard at their marriage of equals, speaking together before the War for abolition and after for women's suffrage. Henry, as well as Lucy, was ridiculed for their relationship. In 1867, a Kansas newspaper editor noted that Lucy Stone and her "poodle" would be arriving to speak on Women's Rights.[12]

Once she married, Lucy began an almost inevitable retreat from life on the lecture circuit, retiring to the sidelines to raise their daughter Alice Stone Blackwell. Yet, she continued to declare her militancy, demonstrating her frustration at women's "taxation without representation" by refusing to pay her real estate taxes in 1858 and letting the house and possessions go to auction while Henry was out of town.

DURING THE WAR, women of the Sanitary Commission returned home from the front to lecture about the soldiers' needs and revive local patriotism.

When the War began, advocates of women's rights agreed to postpone agitation until the final peace, canceling conventions and devoting their platform to a continuing campaign for total emancipation. In 1863 Lucy returned to politics. With women disappointed in the limits of Lincoln's Emancipation Proclamation, she founded the Women's National Loyal League. Their goal was a constitutional amendment abolishing slavery, to be accomplished by petition, a tool abolitionist women had been using for decades. The *Chicago Times* reflected typical conservative opinion in describing the League as "strong minded women on a rampage," an opinion that proved accurate.[13] In a little more than six months local chapters collected enough signatures to present the Senate with the "Prayer of One Hundred Thousand" in February, 1864. With their goal accomplished in the 13th amendment, the organization disbanded.

After the War Lucy and Henry went back on the lecture circuit to fight for voting rights for blacks and women. In 1870 they developed a new forum, a newspaper called *The Women's Journal,* which documented the suffrage movement until 1931. Too much time during the last decades of Lucy's battle was spent feuding with other women's rights supporters, especially Susan B. Anthony and Elizabeth Cady Stanton, who wanted to split the joint campaign into separate fights for women's and African-Americans' suffrage. Anthony and Stanton literally wrote the book on women's rights. Their *History of Women's Suffrage* gives little credit to Lucy Stone, who deserves to be remembered as a hero of the women's revolution and the Civil War.[14]

ACTIVITIES FOR RE-ENACTORS: GIVE A SPEECH AND ASK PEOPLE TO SIGN A PETITION

The woman lecturer played an important role in the Civil War. If you're outgoing and want to memorize a flowery diatribe, consider giving a speech at a re-enactment event. To attract a crowd you'll need broadside posters nailed to a few walls, plus a tree stump or wooden crate as a makeshift stage.

You'll also need the kind of courage possessed by Angelina Grimké and Lucy Stone. Don't expect too much respect from your audience; female speakers were hardly any more welcome before a mixed group in 1863 than they were in the 1840s. But follow Thomas Wentworth Higginson's advice: find a cause that's larger than you are and you'll forget your nervousness. You can write your own piece or find one in a contemporary newspaper, where editors often printed the whole text of a speech.

You might want to memorize the following speech written by Amelia Jenks Bloomer (1818-1894), an eloquent lecturer also known for her advocacy of women's dress reform. To show how much of a reformist you are, you'll want to wear the Bloomer outfit.

Amelia sent this speech to the Women's Loyal League to be read at a convention. In the last year of the War, as Northern enthusiasm for continued fighting waned, politicians preached compromise with the South. The women of the League refused to accept any peace without total freedom for the slaves. Their major tool for political change was the petition, so after your speech you might want to collect signatures.

A LADY LECTURER of the 1870s giving the expressive gesture so important to the concept of good public speaking at the time. Part of Lucy Stone's effectiveness was her naturalness in keeping gestures to a minimum.

Speech by Amelia Jenks Bloomer, 1864

The women of the North are charged by the press with a lack of zeal and enthusiasm in the war. The charge may be true to some extent. Though for the most part the women of the loyal states are loyal to the government, and in favor of sustaining its every measure for putting down the rebellion, yet they do not I fear enter fully into the spirit of the revolution, or share greatly in the enthusiasm and devotion which sustain the women of the South in their struggle for what they believe, their independence and freedom from oppression. This is owning, doubtless, to the war being waged on soil remote from us, to women having no part in the active contest, and to the deprivation and heart-sorrows it has occasioned them. There are too many who think only of themselves and too little of the sufferings of the soldiers who have volunteered to save their country. While they are willing to give of their time and means to relieve the sick and wounded, they at the same time decry the war, lament the sacrifices and expenditure it occasions, think it should have been prevented by a compromise and long for peace on almost any terms. These think not of the great cause at stake, they care not for the poor slave, think not of the future of our country, and fail to see the hand of God in the movement punishing the nation for sin and leading it up through much suffering and tribulation to a brighter and more glorious destiny.

But there is a class of women who have looked beyond the mere class of arms and the battlefield of the dead and dying, and recognize the necessity and importance of this dark hour of trial to our country. The first cannon fired at Sumter sounded in their ears the death knell of slavery and proclaimed the will of the Almighty to this nation. These have never believed we should have peace or great success until the doom of slavery was irrevocably sealed. That seal has been set. Our noble President has bowed to the will of the Supreme Power and by the guidance and sustaining spirit of that Power will, I trust, lead our country successfully through the great and fearful struggle and place it upon a firm and more enduring basis.

The contest has outlasted the expectation of all, and has cost the nation a vast amount of blood and treasure. It has called into the field a million or more of soldiers, and the number of fathers, brothers and sons slain upon the battlefield and wasted away in camps and hospitals is counted by hundreds of thousands, while its expenses run up to billions. And still the war for the Union, for Freedom, and the integrity of our national boundaries goes forward; and in the hearts of true Union men everywhere the firm resolve has been made that it shall go on until the rebellion is crushed, cost what it may, and continue though it should last as long as did the war which brought our nation into existence.

Now the question for us to consider is: Are we prepared for the further and continued sacrifice? Have we yet more sons and brothers to yield up on the altar of our country? To this question let every loyal woman address herself. . . . I know there are many women in whose hearts the love of country and of justice is strong, and who are willing to incur any loss and make almost any sacrifice rather than that the rebellion should succeed and the chains of the bondsmen be more firmly riveted. If they manifest less enthusiasm than their patriotic brothers it is because they have not so great an opportunity for its exercise. The customs of society do not permit any stormy or noisy manifestation of feeling on the part of woman. But the blood of Revolutionary sires flows as purely in her veins as in those of her favored brothers, and she can feel as deeply, suffer as intensely, and endure as bravely as do they.

But I would have her do more than suffer and endure. I would that she should not only resolve to stand by the government of the Union in its work of defeating the schemes of its enemies, but that she should let her voice be heard. *"Women assist us in our struggle. Speak up and sign our petition to let the government know we advocate unconditional surrender."*[15]

Warrior Eagle

Warrior Eagle, machine appliquéd and pieced by Jean Pearson Stanclift,
machine quilted by Jeanne Zyck,
Lawrence, Kansas, 1999.

Jean's *Warrior Eagle* is an adaptation of a pattern that appeared in several quilts during the 1850s. The eagle's militant stance and the word "Liberty" on its banner reflect the politics of women like Lucy Stone, women who forced discussion of the true meaning of the word. This particular version of the eagle echoes a set and border shown in a quilt on the cover of *The Magazine Antiques* in July, 1933. That quilt, with nine blocks, now belongs to the Shelburne Museum.

Size: 100" x 100"

Four blocks, 36" x 36" finished

Sashing strips and inner border, 3" finished

Outer Border, $9^{1}/_{2}$" finished

FABRIC REQUIREMENTS

TAN PRINT: $8^{1}/_{4}$ yards for background, sawtooth sashing, and outer border

BLUE: 4 yards for eagles, sawtooth sashing, border appliqué (birds), and binding

RED: 3 yards for eagles, star centers, and border swag

YELLOW: 3 yards for eagle, stars, and border detail (tassels)

BACKING: $8^{1}/_{4}$ yards

BATTING: 104" x 104"

CUTTING

- Cut the 4 lengthwise border strips 10" x 104" from tan (a little extra to allow for easing and mitering).

- Cut 4 squares 38" x 38" from tan. Trim to $36^{1}/_{2}$" after the appliqué is complete.

- Trace and cut the appliqué templates and fabrics using the patterns given on pages 16-22, adding $^{1}/_{4}$" seam allowances. Cut the 16 border swags and 4 corner swags, using the template on page 16, after you have pieced the entire top and borders.

- You will need 152 each of the tan and blue triangles (3" finished). To piece the sashing triangles, using the template on page 21, cut 76 squares $3^{7}/_{8}$" x $3^{7}/_{8}$" each of the tan and blue; then cut in half diagonally **or** use the grid method on page 118. If using the grid method, cut fourteen rectangles of fabric (seven tan and seven blue) each $15^{1}/_{2}$" x $11^{3}/_{4}$". On the reverse side of the tan fabric draw a grid of 12 squares, each $3^{7}/_{8}$" square. Cut one square $3^{1}/_{2}$" x $3^{1}/_{2}$" for the center.

- Cut backing fabric into three equal lengths. Piece to create backing (page 118).

- Cut 9 strips $2^{1}/_{4}$" x 42" from blue for binding.

THE QUILT TOP

Appliqué Blocks
1. Fold the background squares in half vertically and horizontally. Press. Position the appliqué pieces on the background squares using the fold lines for placement.

2. Appliqué the pieces using your favorite hand or machine appliqué technique (pages 116-117).

3. Reverse appliqué the shields (page 116).

4. Trim the blocks to $36^{1}/_{2}$" x $36^{1}/_{2}$".

Sawtooth Sashing and Inner Border
1. Using the traditional template method or following the instructions for fast-piecing the triangles using a sawtooth grid (page 118), piece 152 sawtooth squares for the sashing and inner borders.

Sawtooth Squares

2. Join 12 sawtooth squares for the vertical block sashing, referring to the photograph of the quilt for correct orientation of the squares. Press. Sew the sashing between two appliquéd blocks. Press. Repeat for the second vertical sashing for the other two appliqué blocks.

3. Join 12 sawtooth squares for the horizontal block sashing, referring to the photograph of the quilt below for correct orientation of the squares. Press. Repeat. Join these two sashing strips with the $3^1/_2$" square in the middle. Press. Attach the sashing to join the four appliqué blocks. Press.

4. Join 25 sawtooth squares for the left border, referring to the photograph for correct orientation of the squares. Repeat for the right border.

5. Join 27 sawtooth squares for the top border, referring to the illustration for correct orientation of the squares. (Note the orientation of the upper left corner square.) Add to the top edge of the quilt top. Press. Repeat for the bottom edge of the quilt top. (Note the orientation of the lower right corner square.)

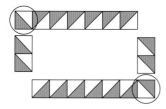

Sashing Placement

6. The quilt top should measure 81" x 81".

Border

Appliqué the swags to the borders before you attach them to the quilt. Do not appliqué the corner swags until after the borders are attached to the quilt top.

1. Position the swags, the birds, and the tassels onto one border strip, referring to the photo on page 13. Appliqué in place.

2. Repeat for the remaining borders.

3. Attach the nearly completed swag borders to the quilt top and miter the corners (page 118). Press.

4. Cut and position the corner swags over the mitered corners, adjusting the length and angle to fit as you cut. Appliqué in place.

QUILTING

1. Layer and baste the quilt (page 119).

2. Jeanne machine quilted the quilt in a curvy all-over pattern. If you want to quilt by hand, you'll probably want to do an all-over design too. One popular mid-century combination is a teacup or orange peel design in the body of the quilt with shells or fans in the borders. You can outline quilt the appliqué or just quilt across it the way nineteenth-century quilters did. If you quilt across the appliqué, you will get a flatter quilt.

3. Bind the quilt (page 119).

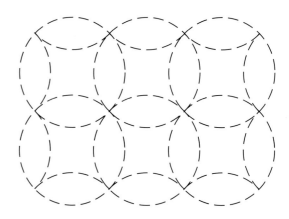

Teacup quilting design of overlapping circles.

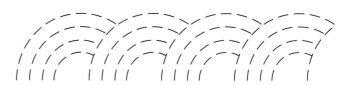

Fan quilting for the border.

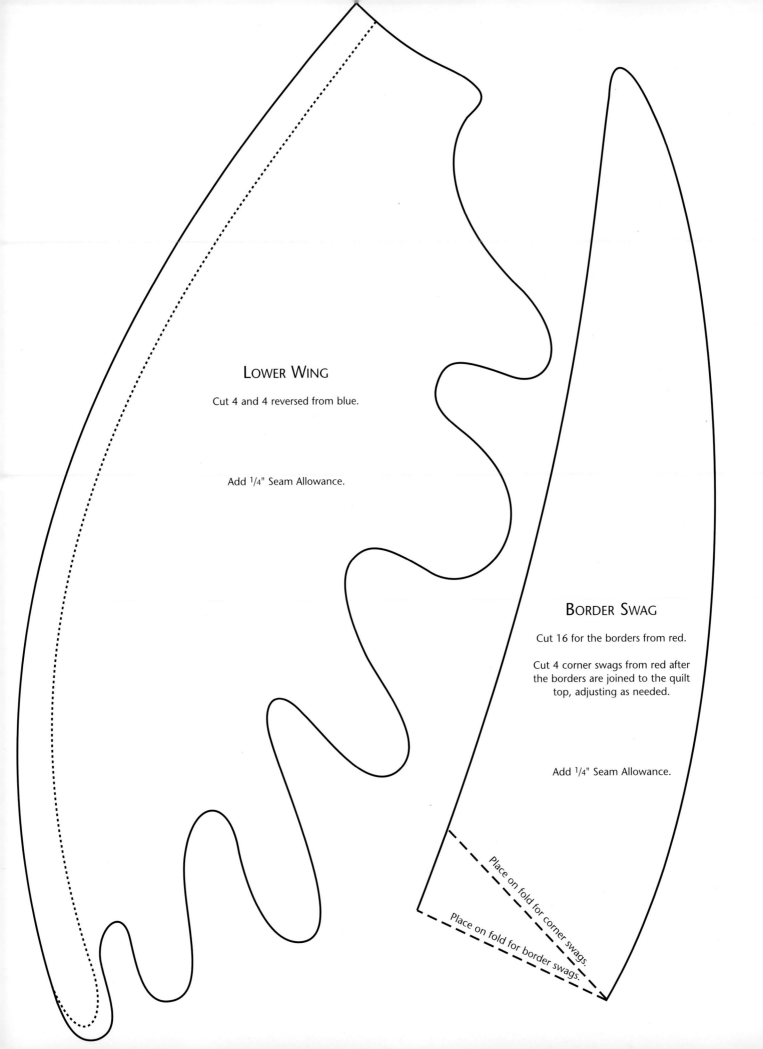

LOWER WING

Cut 4 and 4 reversed from blue.

Add ¼" Seam Allowance.

BORDER SWAG

Cut 16 for the borders from red.

Cut 4 corner swags from red after
the borders are joined to the quilt
top, adjusting as needed.

Add ¼" Seam Allowance.

Place on fold for corner swags.

Place on fold for border swags.

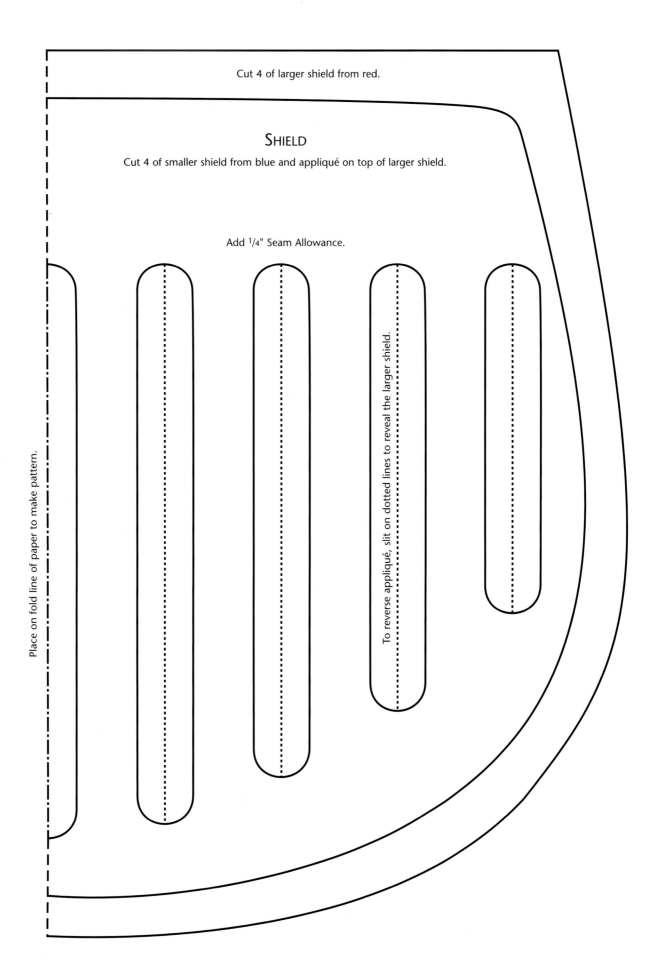

Cut 4 of larger shield from red.

SHIELD

Cut 4 of smaller shield from blue and appliqué on top of larger shield.

Add ¼" Seam Allowance.

To reverse appliqué, slit on dotted lines to reveal the larger shield.

Place on fold line of paper to make pattern.

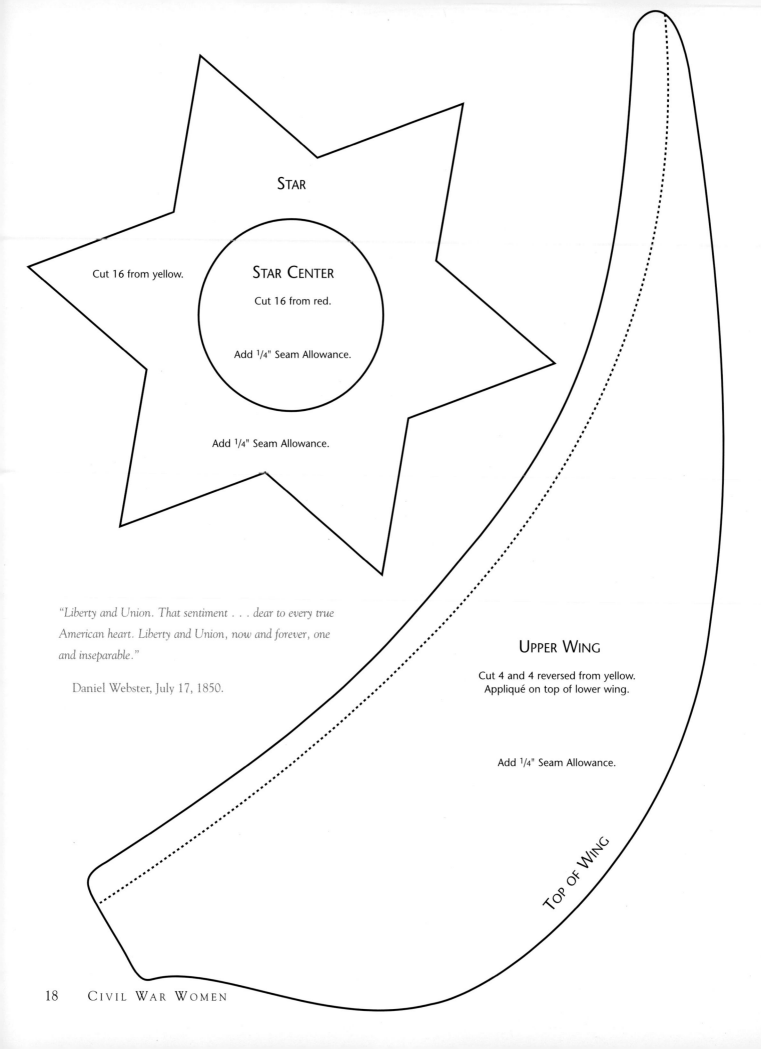

STAR

Cut 16 from yellow.

STAR CENTER

Cut 16 from red.

Add 1/4" Seam Allowance.

Add 1/4" Seam Allowance.

"Liberty and Union. That sentiment . . . dear to every true American heart. Liberty and Union, now and forever, one and inseparable."

Daniel Webster, July 17, 1850.

UPPER WING

Cut 4 and 4 reversed from yellow.
Appliqué on top of lower wing.

Add 1/4" Seam Allowance.

TOP OF WING

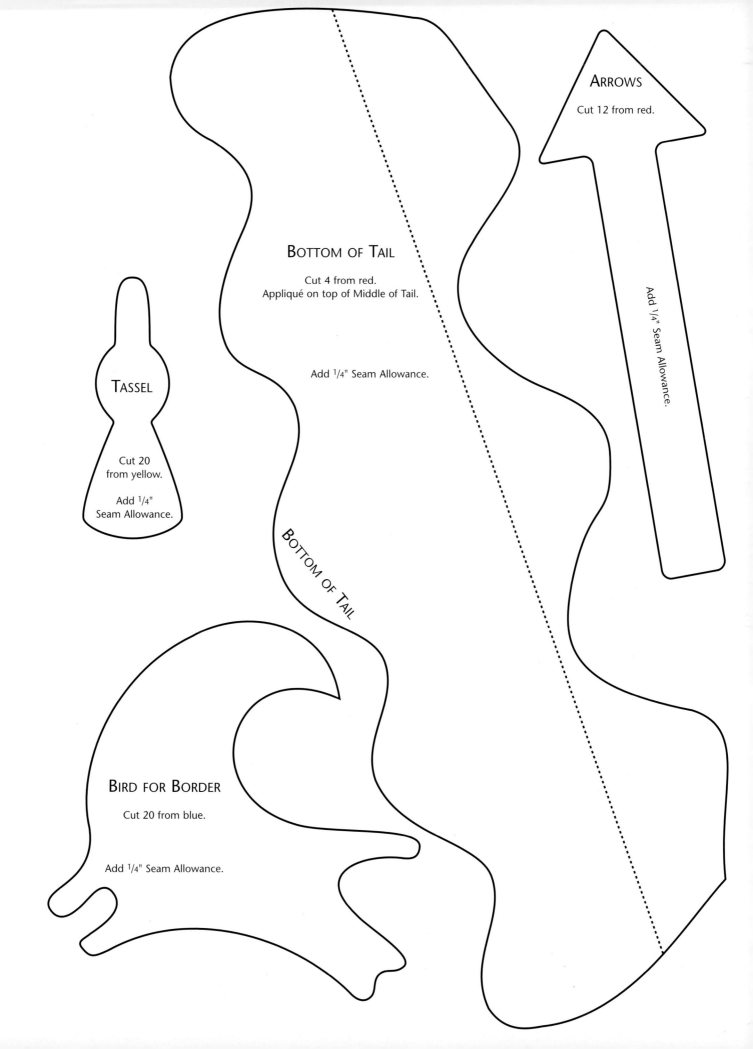

ARROWS

Cut 12 from red.

BOTTOM OF TAIL

Cut 4 from red.
Appliqué on top of Middle of Tail.

Add ¹/₄" Seam Allowance.

Add ¹/₄" Seam Allowance.

TASSEL

Cut 20
from yellow.

Add ¹/₄"
Seam Allowance.

BOTTOM OF TAIL

BIRD FOR BORDER

Cut 20 from blue.

Add ¹/₄" Seam Allowance.

Embroider, ink, or appliqué the word Liberty.

Link this to the beak with a strip of 1/2" bias.

BANNER

Cut 4 from yellow.

LIBERTY

Add 1/4" Seam Allowance.

MIDDLE OF TAIL

Cut 4 from yellow.

Add 1/4" Seam Allowance.

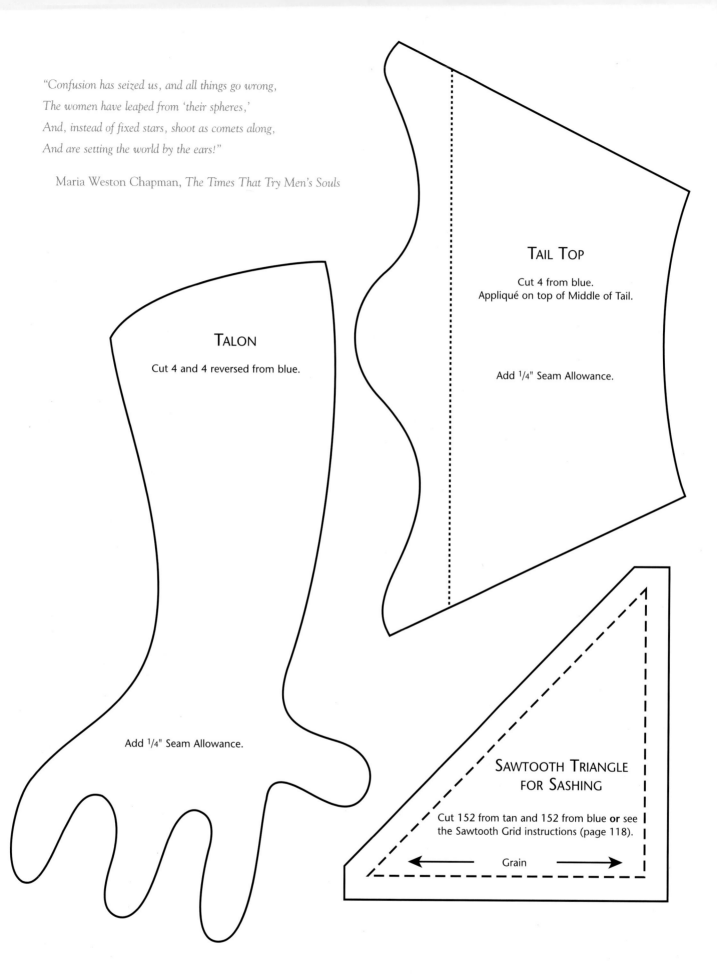

"Confusion has seized us, and all things go wrong,
The women have leaped from 'their spheres,'
And, instead of fixed stars, shoot as comets along,
And are setting the world by the ears!"

Maria Weston Chapman, *The Times That Try Men's Souls*

TAIL TOP

Cut 4 from blue.
Appliqué on top of Middle of Tail.

Add ¼" Seam Allowance.

TALON

Cut 4 and 4 reversed from blue.

Add ¼" Seam Allowance.

SAWTOOTH TRIANGLE
FOR SASHING

Cut 152 from tan and 152 from blue **or** see
the Sawtooth Grid instructions (page 118).

← Grain →

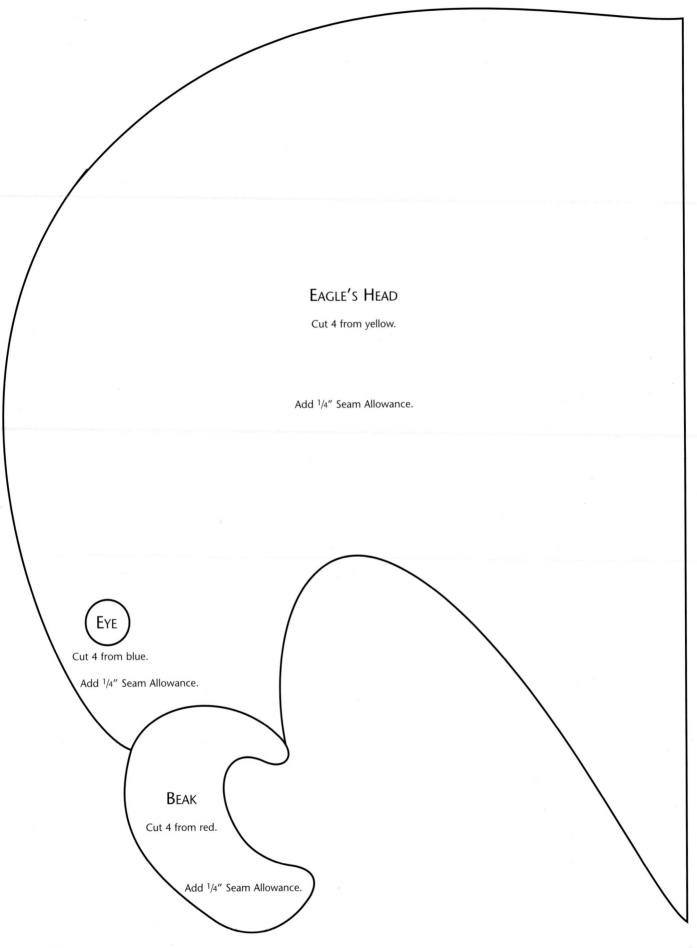

EAGLE'S HEAD

Cut 4 from yellow.

Add ¼" Seam Allowance.

EYE

Cut 4 from blue.

Add ¼" Seam Allowance.

BEAK

Cut 4 from red.

Add ¼" Seam Allowance.

CHAPTER 2

REMEMBERING SUSIE KING TAYLOR AND OTHER FREEDWOMEN

January 27, 1861 Dear Miss Mary,

We had a fine time last night with just our own people and Payton to play the violin and banjo, and Simon played on the tambourine. Susan had a quilting and after we got the quilt out they had to dance instead of a supper . . . I have sent for a barrel [of flour]. I will have my quilting next Saturday night. I want my flour to come so I may have a supper. . . . Milly has not grown six inches since you went away. She sends a heap of howdy to you. . . .

Your affectionate servant, Martha Watkins."[16]

What kinds of quilts might slaves have made? Freedwoman Martha Colquitt of Georgia remembered that "Grandma . . . used to piece up a heap of quilts out of our old clothes and any kind of scraps she could get a hold of. I don't know what the others had in their cabins because Ma didn't allow her children to visit round the other folks."

Too many quilt fans imagine that all slave-made quilts were alike: scrappy quilts of old clothes, quickly pieced together for warmth. Surviving quilts with reliable stories of origins in slavery reflect the varying aesthetics of the time—pieced designs of calicoes, chintzes, and ginghams or red and green floral appliqués. Some are simply done, while others are quite elaborate, such as *broderie perse* medallions cut of English and French chintzes.[17]

A quilt search in Wyandotte County, Kansas, turned up an example of tattered elegance that indicates the broad range of slave-made quilts. We call the pattern "Feathered Star," but the name handed down in its white family is "Tobacco Worm," an apt description for little green sawtooth triangles that resemble the horny green worm. The present owner inherited the quilt from her grandmother who married a man from Kentucky during the Civil War at 16. Her husband brought to Kansas a freedman, Mr. Rhodes, whose grandmother made the quilt before the War. The family was surprised when the quilt documenters called it Feathered Star.

We know little about slave-made quilts because we have so few first-person accounts. Slaves were forbidden to learn to read and write, so letters and diaries from women in slavery are rare. One remarkable small group of dictated letters from women on the Watkins plantation in Mississippi survive. Martha dictated the letter above to her owner Sarah E. Watkins, who sent it with other "howdies" from the slave women to daughter Mary, who was away at school.

Previous page

THE PARADE BANNER, copied by Mary Wilk Madden from an antique, bears a message that's easy to decipher, but did the old star quilts carry a message too? We call the pattern "Feathered Star," but what did the nineteenth-century quiltmakers call them?

Martha and her sister slaves give us insight into the role of quiltmaking in slaves' social lives as the war began. On the Watkins plantation, quiltings were common. As in other American cultures, Martha and Susan probably each pieced or appliquéd a quilt top, then invited friends to quilt the layers together in what later generations called a quilting bee. Martha notes that the men played music while the women stitched at the frame. Rather than serving her guests a meal when the quilting was finished, Susan substituted dancing, an indication that she had little extra money for food for company. Martha must have been better off; she planned to serve supper with the flour that the women were permitted to buy for bread and biscuits. Polly, a fellow slave at the Watkins home, also dictated a note about her planned quilting. "While they have dancing in their heads they must take it as their supper. I am too poor to give us supper. I have one half a barrel of flour coming, but I must keep it for my fatherless children."[19]

In the 1930s, writers working for the federal W.P.A. (Work Projects Administration) recorded the memories of former slaves. Marriah Hines recalled her days on a Virginia plantation rather idyllically, possibly telling the white interviewer just what she wanted to hear. "Evenings we would spin on the old spinning wheel, quilt, make clothes, talk, tell jokes and a few had learned to weave a little bit from the missus." Fannie Moore of North Carolina recalled no jokes when she told of quilting in her youth. "My mammy worked in the field all day and pieced and quilted all night. Then she had to spin enough thread to make four cuts for the white folks every night [a cut is a measurement of spun yarn]. Why sometime I never go to bed. Have to hold the light for her to see by. She had to piece quilts for the white folks too. . . . I never see how my mammy stood such hard work."

A letter from plantation owner Mary Jones to her daughter in 1861 echoes the idea of "making" a slave do the work. "Tell my dear little granddaughter Grandma sends a little quilt for her bed. I wanted to have quilted it this summer, but there is no prospect now. I had nothing new to bind it, but send a curtain (not old, but stained with mildew); it will answer very well, and perhaps you could make Lucy [a slave] quilt it, if not run the two together."[20]

Kate Stone talked about a quilting at her house in Louisiana when the women who usually worked in the fields found easier work. "Mamma had several of the women from the quarter sewing. Nothing to be done in the fields—too muddy. They put in and finished quilting a comfort made of two of my cashmere dresses. Mamma had Aunt Laura's silk one put in today and Sue is quilting on it."[21]

We know about the lives of slave quiltmakers primarily through the written words of their white owners or the interviewers who talked to them towards the end of their lives. Yet several ex-slaves left first-person accounts of their lives before and after emancipation, among them Susie King Taylor (1848 - ?).

"I asked Philis if she liked the thought of being free. She said yes, though she had always been treated with perfect kindness and could complain of nothing in her lot, but she had heard a woman who had bought her freedom from kind indulgent owners, say it was a very sweet thing to be able to do as she chose, to sit and do nothing, to work if she desired or to go out as she liked and ask nobody's permission."

Grace Brown Elmore.
May 24, 1865.[18]

A WASHERWOMAN continues her work while the Christian Commission serves coffee.

In Spring, 1862, Union troops near Savannah, Georgia, declared that slaves in their vicinity would be offered freedom and protection. Susie Baker was one of the first slaves to be officially freed, a year before Lincoln's Emancipation Proclamation. She was fourteen years old when her uncle brought his family to sanctuary. The family went to Saint Simon's Island, where Susie was a laundress for the army. She had skills more valuable than bleaching and starching, however. She'd learned to read and write as a child in Savannah. Her grandmother had sent her to a secret school conducted by a free woman of color. With two dozen other slave children, Susie sneaked into the school daily, ". . . [their] books wrapped in paper to prevent the police or white persons from seeing them."[22]

In South Carolina, as in most of the slave states, a statute forbade teaching slaves to write, threatening violators with a large fine. Sarah Grimké remembered as a child, "I took an almost malicious satisfaction in teaching my little waiting-maid at night, when she was supposed to be occupied in combing and brushing my long locks. The light was put out, the keyhole screened, and flat on our stomachs, before the fire, with the spelling-book under our eyes, we defied the laws of South Carolina."[23]

On St. Simon's Island Susie taught many of the six hundred freed slaves who had been denied literacy. She soon married Edward King, a sergeant in the African-American troops organized along the Georgia and Carolina coasts. In marrying so young, Susie maintained a family pattern. Her mother and her grandmother delivered their first children at age fourteen. Sgt. Edward King served under Thomas Wentworth Higginson, Lucy Stone's Boston friend, who organized freedmen into fighting troops in the Sea Islands. When the men marched south to fight in Florida, Susie accompanied the 33rd U.S. Colored Troops of South Carolina Volunteers as a nurse, a role she learned as Clara Barton's assistant in the eight months Barton spent on the islands.

Edward survived the War, only to die in an accident in Savannah in 1866. He left his eighteen-year-old wife, as she worded it in her autobiography, "to welcome a little stranger alone." She raised her child by teaching school when she could find paying pupils and by doing housework and laundry for women in Savannah and Boston. Thirteen years later Susie married Russell Taylor. In her memoirs she tells us little about her post-War life, but mentions that she was active in the Veterans' organizations, especially the Women's Relief Corps, the auxiliary of the Grand Army of the Republic (G.A.R.). She recalled an 1898 ladies' fair for the G.A.R. in which she showed "a large quilt of red, white and blue ribbon that made quite a sensation."

Susie was of the generation of freed slaves who lived through extraordinary times. They endured slavery, believed in the promises of emancipation, and made the best of the degradation of Reconstruction to survive into the 20th century. She spoke for her generation at the close of her memoirs: "Can we forget these cruelties? No, though we try to forgive and say, 'No North, no South' and hope to see it in reality before the last comrade passes away."

"November 16, 1862.

Cut out a dress to-day for an old woman—Venus—who thanked and blessed me enough, poor old soul. It was a pleasure to hear her say what a happy year this has been for her: 'Nobody to whip me nor drive me, and plenty to eat. Never had such a happy year in my life before.' 'Promised to make a little dress for her great-grandchild—only a few weeks old. It shall be a bright pink calico, such as will delight the little free baby's eyes.'"[24]

MEDALLION QUILT TOP, maker unknown, ca. 1840-1865, 98" x 72".

I bought this top because I wanted a mid-century medallion quilt. The dealer assured me I was buying a quilt made by an African-American woman. She could prove it, she said, and told me all the myths about African-American quilt-making as she pointed to the haphazard needlework and randomness of the pattern. When I protested that this was typical of everyday quilts of the era and that African-American women made a wide variety of quilts, some quite elegant, she told me that I needed to read more about African-American quilts. I bought the quilt despite its confusing origins. I have no idea who made it and feel confident that no one could accurately determine the race, ethnic origins, or occupation of the maker from this quilt's appearance.

MEMBERS OF THE CHRISTIAN COMMISSION pose with barrels of their supplies for soldiers in camp. The hierarchy of black and white continued long after freedom.

ACTIVITY FOR RE-ENACTORS: PUT ON A QUILTING PARTY

We call them "Quilting Bees," but during the Civil War, the name was "Quilting Frolic," "Quilting Party," or just plain "Quilting." These get-togethers were popular all over the United States with more similarities than differences between a quilting party of Massachusetts blue-stockings (lady intellectuals) or Kentucky slaveholders. Southern women in slavery seem to have held parties similar to those of their owners, although with less abundance at the table.

Quilting parties make ideal outdoor events. A quilt stretched in a wooden frame under a tree invites strangers to sit down and become friends. If you have a tent and can keep the frame up and the quilters stitching for a long weekend, you'll probably get your quilt top finished. In the old days women quilted a top in one hard-working eight-hour day.

To stage a quilting party, you'll need a quilt top, a frame, food, and a fiddler. Provide your quilters with plenty of needles, thimbles, scissors, and thread. Wooden spools would be nice. If you have any old ones, you might rewind your new thread from today's plastic spools onto the wooden ones. Bring a little basket to throw the thread clippings in. You'll need to teach the novices how to sew quilting stitches, but you'll be surprised how many experienced quilters you'll find. They'll help you explain hiding the knots, using a thimble, and pacing stitches so they are even on top and bottom.

I am assuming you know how to mark, baste, and put a quilt in a frame. If not, refer to a basic hand quilting book such as *Hand Quilting with Alex Anderson*.

The Quilting Party
When I Saw Sweet Nelly Home
"In the sky the bright stars glittered,
On the grass the moonlight fell,
Hushed the sound of daylight bustle
Closed the Pinkeyed Pimpernell.
As a down the moss grown woodpath
Where the cattle love to roam
From Aunt Dinah's quilting party
I was seeing Nellie home."

A popular song by Frances Kyle and J. Fletcher, 1856.

THE WEEK THE WAR BROKE OUT, *Harper's Weekly* featured "Quilting" among "American Home Scenes" by Winslow Homer. Two women prepare a meal for seven quilters of varying ages, who stitch a quilt in a frame propped on straight back chairs. Would dancing partners and musicians drop in later?

For instructions on hosting the party, read these descriptions of mid-century quilting parties North and South.

"[In Illinois] The women held quilting parties. A patchwork quilt was generally prepared thus for quilting: The lining was first placed in frames made for the purpose, the cotton laid smoothly over the lining, then the patchwork spread over and basted closely all around the edges. Then, with chalk and line, the women marked out the quilting. . . . among so many there were often drones or unskilled needlewomen. These went into the kitchen and helped the housewife cook the dinner and supper, an indispensable feature of the occasion. The young people many times remained for dancing or games, according to the scruples of the persons giving the entertainment." [25]

"[In Texas] I recall spending a very enjoyable day at a quilting bee. While the fingers plied the needle, tongues were equally busy. At noon all repaired to the dining room, which also served as a kitchen. The table groaned under the burden of rations tempting to the appetite. The feast lasted as long as we were there. When twilight began to fall the young men gathered in for a dance. And a dance it was. Few indulged in the round dance; the old time square dance was most popular. . . . The beverage was steaming hot coffee. The dance lasted until daylight." [26]

"[In North Carolina] I have been to —Ford since the first of September until last Monday I came home. The people there is so hide[bound] between religion and the thoughts of high[life] that you may know that I did not have much satisfaction. I was to four quiltings, but not any _dancing_ at one of them." Letter from Ginny Alexander to Mary Springs, 1803. [27]

"[In New Hampshire] Swiftly the needles flew, and the tongues, too, until tea, which in those old-fashioned times was at precisely 5 o'clock. . . . the tiny cups . . . were filled with the best Souchong and cream and sugar added to suit before passing. There were the delicate cream biscuits right from the oven, the golden butter, custard pies, currant tarts, plum preserves, honey, cheese, and of course the 'election cake,' which to the uninitiated, may be better known as 'riz' with raisins in it. . . . At sundown the quilt is finished and taken from the frame, and each matron is on her homeward way." "Hope Harvest" for Johnson's Lake Shore Home Magazine, 1883. [28]

"[In Kentucky or Tennessee] Mrs Rapp, her daughter Angelina, her white help Clementina and her borrowed slave Lily, labour unremittingly throughout the day to prepare for the tea in the best style of quilting frolic liberality. . . . By about 5 o'clock all is completed; Mrs. Rapp and her daughter are full dressed in the keeping room; whiskey, water, sugar and tumblers, are ranged upon the sideboard." [29] Frances Trollope, 1832.

"[In Texas] The quilt was stretched in the primitive way, that is between 4 slats and drawn out to the full size of the quilt—and the four corners each suspended by a rope to the ceiling—in the best room. Now all the ladies are expected to come early as the quilt has to be finished before the real fun begins. . . . The gents on the ground are expected to roll up the sides as fast as needed, to pass the thread and scissors—and with anecdotes and small talk to entertain the workers. In the meantime things are getting hot in the kitchen, the biggest Turkey on the place is basting his back before a huge log fire. A little porker had folded his feet under him and laid down in the bottom of a great Oven. . . . Pies and cakes of all sizes . . . chickens, eggs, butter, milk, preserves &c . . . The shades of night have settled upon the scene, ere the fragments of the feast are cleared away—but the sound of the violin expedites further preparations—and now change your partners and we'll all dance a reel." C. C. Cox. [30]

"[In New England] Here is the memento of a mischievous brother, who was determined to assist, otherwise than by his legitimate occupation of rolling up the quilt as it was finished, snapping the chalk-line, passing thread, wax and scissors, and shaking hands across the quilt for all girls with short arms. He must take the thread and needle. We gave him white thread, and appointed him to a very dark piece of calico, so that we might pick it out the easier; but there! to spite us, he did it so nicely that it still remains." Anonymous. 1845. [31]

"[In Louisiana] Mamma had Aunt Laura's silk [quilt] put in today and Sue [a slave] is quilting on it. I am so afraid Mamma will commence work on it herself, and if she does I shall feel in duty bound to put up my linen embroidery and help her. And I simply detest making and quilting quilts. . . . After quilting one rises from the chair with such a backache, headache and bleeding pricked fingers." Kate Stone, 1861. [32]

Tobacco Worm

Tobacco Worm (Feathered Star), machine pieced and
machine appliquéd by Cherie Ralston,
Lawrence, Kansas, 1999.

Cherie's quilt is an adaptation of one attributed by its current owners, to a woman in slavery. Cherie redrafted the Feathered Star pattern and added a border inspired by the original, which was a full-sized quilt made in the colors typical for best quilts of 1840-1865. The stars were green with an occasional piece of brown; the appliquéd borders were red, green, and bright chrome yellow; and of course the feathers, the little triangles on the edge of the stars, were the exact yellow-green of a tobacco worm. Cherie used softer colors, browns and brick reds that echo antique fabrics. You might want to make a full-sized quilt by piecing four of the 34" blocks together, and adapting the border for a larger quilt, which will be 90" square.

Feathered Stars are among the most difficult patterns to draft. The major problem is the feathers, those pesky tobacco worms. There are two sets of triangles in the feathers and two sets of squares (what Cherie calls A and B). Most people don't notice the differences, because the measurements vary only by $1/8$" in this pattern. That fraction is the key to accuracy, however, so be sure you understand where to piece one set of triangles and squares (A) and the other (B) before you begin cutting.

Size: 56" x 56"

Central block, 34" x 34" finished

Narrow border, 1" finished

Appliquéd border, 10" finished

FABRIC REQUIREMENTS

TAN SOLID: $1/2$ yard

TWO TAN PRINTS: $3/4$ yard for the star, $1^1/2$ yards for the outer border

MEDIUM BROWN PRINT: $1/2$ yard

DARK BROWN PRINT: 2 yards for the star, inner border, and outer border appliqués

TWO RED PRINTS: $3/4$ yard for the star, 12" x 12" scrap for the outer border appliqués

BACKING: $3^3/4$ yards

BATTING: 60" x 60"

BINDING: $1/2$ yard

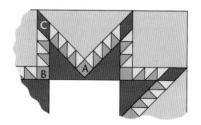

Notice that some of the rows of feathers run parallel to the edge of the block (B) and others run at a diagonal (A). These two lines of feathers meet at the diamond (C), which does not have equal sides. On two sides it is 3" and matches up to A; on the other two sides it is $2^7/8$" and matches up to B. Be careful to keep your diamonds going the right direction. (Template on page 35.)

CUTTING

- Cut 4 squares $6^7/8$" x $6^7/8$" from the red print for the star. Then cut each square in half diagonally (D).

- Cut one square $12^1/2$" x $12^1/2$" from the dark brown print (E).

- Cut 4 squares $9^1/2$" x $9^1/2$" from the tan print for the star (F).

- Cut one square $17^1/4$" x $17^1/4$" from the tan print. Then cut it in half diagonally twice (G).

After you have cut the larger pieces, cut the "feathers" from the tan solid, red print, and medium brown print, using the templates on page 34.

- Cut 4 using template C on page 35 from the red print for the star. Then cut 4 more, reversed.

- Cut 4 using template A and 4 using template B on page 34 from the medium brown print (note the grain lines on the templates). Make a note of which are A and which are B by writing on the back of each.

- Cut 24 using template A1 and 16 using template B1 on page 34 from the medium brown print. Again label these on the back as you cut them, because they are so easily confused.

- Cut 32 using template A1 and 24 using template B1 on page 34 from the tan solid. Label them on the back.

- Cut two lengthwise strips $1\frac{1}{2}"$ x 35" and two lengthwise strips $1\frac{1}{2}"$ x 37" from the dark brown print for the inner border.

- Cut two strips $10\frac{1}{2}"$ x 37" and two strips $10\frac{1}{2}"$ x 57" from the tan print for the outer border.

- Cut the appliqué pieces from the templates on page 35 as indicated, adding $\frac{1}{4}"$ seam allowances.

- Cut the backing fabric into two equal lengths. Piece to create backing (page 118).

- Cut 6 strips $2\frac{1}{4}"$ x 42" for the binding.

THE QUILT TOP

Feathered Star

1. Join 5 B1 triangles. Add one B square to this unit. Add one D triangle (BD). Make 4 and 4 reversed, following the illustration.

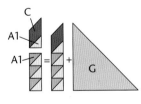

Step 1

2. Join 6 A1 triangles. Join one light A1 triangle to a C diamond. Join the 2 units. Add one G triangle to this unit.

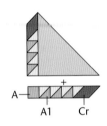

Step 2

3. Join 6 A1 triangles. Join one light A1 triangle to a C reversed diamond. Add one A square following the illustration. Add this unit to the other side of the G triangle. Make 2.

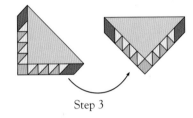

Step 3

4. Join two D units to a G unit. Make 2.

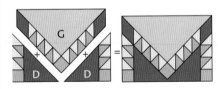

Step 4

5. Join 4 B1 triangles. Join one light B1 triangle to a C diamond. Join the 2 units. Add one F square. Make 2 and 2 reversed.

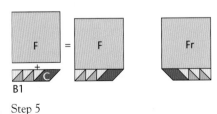

Step 5

6. Join one F and one F reversed unit to one DG unit. Make 2.

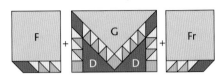

Step 6

7. Join 7 A1 triangles. Add one A square to this unit. Add this unit to the bias edge of one D triangle.

8. Join 7 A1 triangles. Add to the A square of the unit pieced in Step 7.

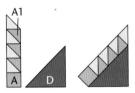

Step 7

Step 8

9. Add the bias edge of one D triangle to this unit as shown. Make 2.

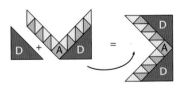

Step 9

10. Join the two units pieced in Step 9 to two sides of the E square. Make 1.

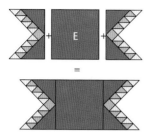

Step 10

11. Join the rows as shown in the illustration.

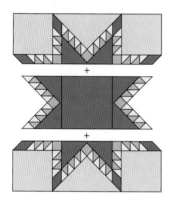

Step 11

12. Set in the G triangles, sewing from the center to the edge on each side of the triangle.

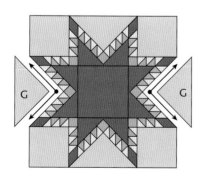

Step 12

Borders

Inner Border

1. Add the shorter $1^1/2$" inner border strips to the sides of the quilt top. Press.

2. Add the longer border strips to the top and bottom. Press.

3. Trim to 37" x 37".

Outer Border

1. Find the centers of the $10^1/2$" border strips and place a set of three leaves there (using one red for the center leaf and the other red for the two outer leaves) as shown in the quilt photograph.

2. Arrange the side and corner swags.

3. Appliqué the swags and leaves, but do not appliqué the center leaf in each border, as that overlaps the dark brown corner border. And do not appliqué the corner leaves until later.

4. Complete the border appliqué except for the corners, and add the outer border strips to the quilt top. Press.

5. Place the leaves over the seams and finish the appliqué. Press.

6. Trim the quilt to 54" x 54".

QUILTING

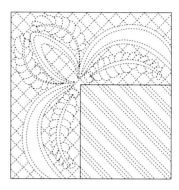

1. Layer and baste the quilt (page 119).

2. If you like to hand quilt, this little piece is a great place for masterpiece quilting. The sketch shows the quilting on the original, which we can imagine was finished by a group of quilters rather than only one. They quilted the star block in triple diagonal lines $1/4$" apart, then skipped a $1/2$" space and quilted three more lines. In the border they outline quilted the appliquéd pieces and quilted feathers on the inside of the swags and the outside of the corner swags. They filled in behind the feathers with a diagonal $3/4$" grid. Triple-line quilting, feathers, and filler grids make for a lot of quilting, but if you want authentic-looking reproductions, it's worth the investment of time.

3. Bind the quilt (page 119).

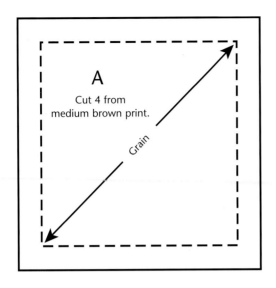

A

Cut 4 from
medium brown print.

Grain

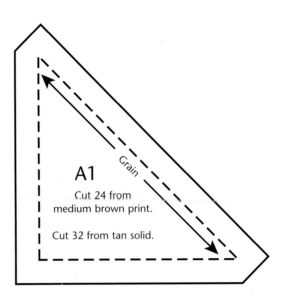

A1

Cut 24 from
medium brown print.

Cut 32 from tan solid.

Grain

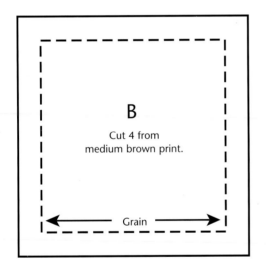

B

Cut 4 from
medium brown print.

Grain

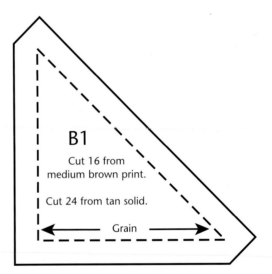

B1

Cut 16 from
medium brown print.

Cut 24 from tan solid.

Grain

*"She said that all her family were slaves in
Old Virginia. Once, because her husband had
carelessly passed by some tobacco worms on
a plant, the new master attempted to beat him.
She and her son jumped into the fray and
stopped him. For so doing all were flogged."[33]*

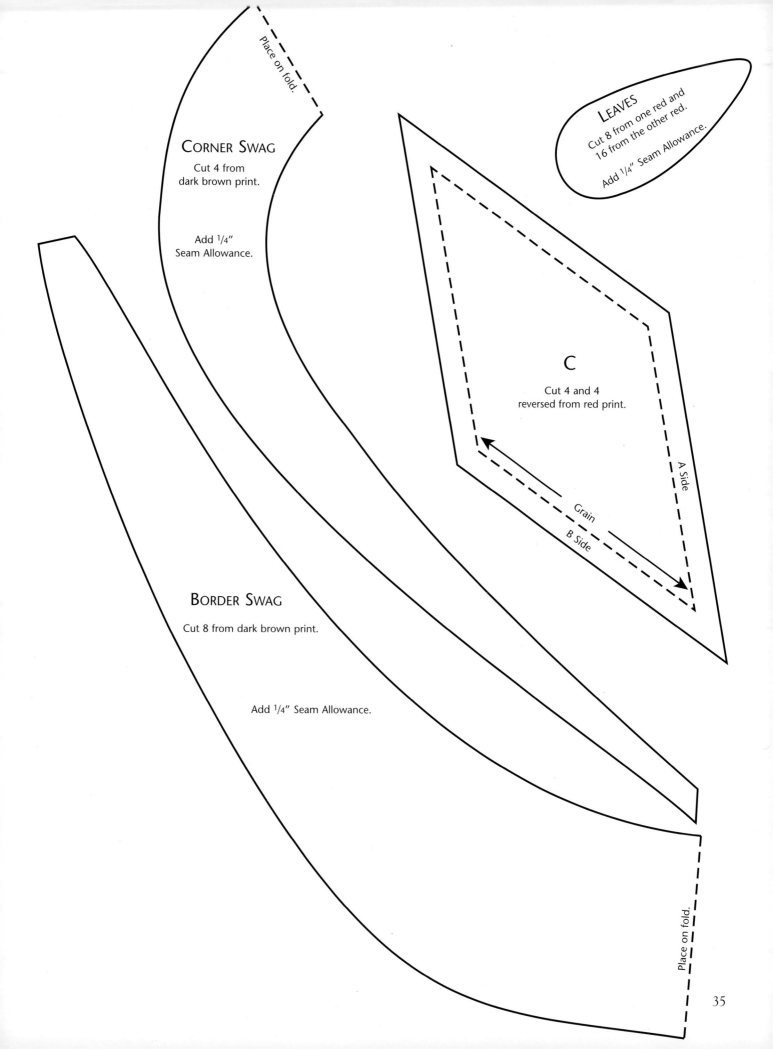

Place on fold.

CORNER SWAG
Cut 4 from
dark brown print.

Add ¼″
Seam Allowance.

LEAVES
Cut 8 from one red and
16 from the other red.

Add ¼″ Seam Allowance.

C
Cut 4 and 4
reversed from red print.

A Side

Grain

B Side

BORDER SWAG
Cut 8 from dark brown print.

Add ¼″ Seam Allowance.

Place on fold.

CHAPTER 3

REMEMBERING JULIA LOUISA LOVEJOY AND OTHER NEWSPAPER CORRESPONDENTS

"Kansas will be saved, we believe . . . I tell you all tho we have felt the horrors of war, if we were not in Kansas already we would come as soon as steam could bring us. Dear Edith's death is the only drawback. Come on all who can."

   Julia Lovejoy, December 9, 1856.

"Kansas Troubles," a time-honored quilt pattern, recalls Julia Hardy Lovejoy (1812-1882), one of the exclusive corps of female Civil War correspondents. Julia began her newspaper career in 1855 describing the "troubles" in Kansas. Editors, desperate for news from "Bleeding Kansas," printed letters from amateur and professional journalists alike. Americans in both North and South devoured columns of print about the private armies of free-state militia and pro-slavery troops battling over the question of whether the territory would come into the Union free or slave. Correspondents rushed to the new towns of Lawrence, Topeka, and Fort Scott to telegraph reports signed with pen names like "Worcester," "Hiawatha," or "One Who's Been There." Papers published rumors and lies as truth, but the truth in Kansas was sensational enough. Settlers massacred each other, armies of vigilantes burned towns, and abolitionists established a revolutionary government parallel to the pro-slavery government favored by the President. Richard J. Hinton, a correspondent for the *Boston Traveller*, lauded the pen as an effective weapon, as valuable as any Sharp's Rifle or Colt's Revolver. Few correspondents claimed neutrality. James Redpath, of the New York *Tribune*, wrote that he'd gone to Kansas with "my pen to precipitate a revolution."[34]

Julia Louisa Hardy Lovejoy's politics were anti-slavery. She was born in New Hampshire, an enthusiastic Methodist from her conversion at a camp meeting when she was sixteen years old. Among the other converts was a childhood friend, Charles H. Lovejoy, born a Baptist, but inspired to preach the Methodist doctrine at eighteen years of age. Julia spent years looking for her spiritual duty. She became a milliner's apprentice and a teacher, but on her nineteenth birthday she confided to her diary that she felt called to save souls. "I dare not tell my feelings to anyone, lest mine be an isolated case. It does not seem that other females are so strangely exercised in mind, in this matter." When she was twenty-four she agreed to marry Charles, who long "had placed his affections on Julia," even though she knew how difficult the life of a Methodist minister's wife would be.[35]

"We go to rear a wall of men
On Freedom's Southern line
And plant beside the cotton trees
The rugged Northern Pine."

Previous page

THE PEN AND THE PRINTING PRESS rallied Americans to the anti-slavery cause of pre-Civil War Kansas. "Kansas Troubles" quilts by Pamela Mayfield and Rosie Mayhew (page 38) recall the days of Bleeding Kansas. Rosie's border of New England Pine Trees and Kansas Cottonwoods was inspired by John Greenleaf Whittier's poem, "The Song of the Kansas Immigrant." Project instructions for this quilt begin on page 42.

KANSAS TROUBLES, machine pieced by Karla Carney Menaugh and machine quilted by Cherie Ralston, Lawrence, Kansas, 1998
84" x 84".
Karla and Cherie challenged each other to make a quilt from a single line of reproduction fabric. The only exception is the binding, an afterthought. Karla used sixteen 16" blocks and divided her prints into darks, mediums, and lights. The soft shades, the scrappy look, and the large-scale print in the 10" border give the quilt a mid-century air. It might have been made when Julia Lovejoy was describing the "Kansas Troubles" for readers back in the states.

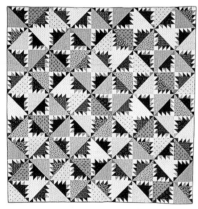

KANSAS TROUBLES, machine pieced and machine quilted by Pamela Mayfield, Lawrence, Kansas, 1999
90" x 90".
Pam's version of the Kansas Troubles, using a different block, focuses on reproduction prints for an old-fashioned effect, contrasting several neutral shades just as nineteenth-century quilters often did.

The Lovejoys spent much of their lives on the Methodist circuit, moving annually as directed by his Conference, surviving in genteel poverty on the generosity of the flock. Charles's duties called him for weeks on end, leaving Julia alone and terribly lonely, complaining to her diary about his absence at events from Thanksgiving dinner to labor and childbirth. In the spring of 1855, Charles, a very pregnant Julia, and their three children were bound for Kansas with a mission to minister to the Methodists in the new Territory. Like many other clergy there, they also hoped to further the abolitionist cause. Julia arranged to describe their journey in letters to several New Hampshire newspapers and the New York *Tribune*.

The Lovejoys were soldiers in an army of immigrants, mustered in by New England anti-slavery organizations that used every propaganda technique available at the time. Chief among these was poetry. Miriam Warner Brewster of Massachusetts also decided that her family should go to Kansas. "What are our convictions and words worth if they bring not action to prove them earnest?" As she spent the summer packing, she kept up her spirits by humming free-state poetry set to music. Kansas pioneers marched to the train station singing the words of poems like John Greenleaf Whittier's "Song of the Kansas Immigrant." Whittier's imagery linked the spirit of the Revolution to the new battleground (the prairie) and New England's symbol of strength and liberty (the pine tree).[36]

Miriam Brewster and Julia Lovejoy needed all the courage of their religious and political convictions to make the move west. Julia's frontier experiences testify to a faith that rarely permitted her to despair. After arriving by river in Kansas City, Charles and their son rode ahead one hundred miles west to homestead land in the new free-state settlement of Manhattan. In trade for room and board, Julia and her fifteen-year-old daughter Juliette waited tables at a rough hotel. The sanitation was so poor that Julia, Juliette, and five-year-old Edith became ill. Realizing that waiting for Charles in Kansas City could prove fatal, Julia wired her husband to return immediately. She found passage on a west-bound riverboat. Like many boats navigating the shallow Kansas River, the *Financier* ran aground and stayed aground. On the stranded boat, as Edith suffered through the measles, Julia hired a wagon and driver to get the family to Lawrence, the Territory's free-state capital. The trip was a nightmare. The boarding house landlady, the teamster, and the other frontier Kansans horrified the New England minister's wife with their tempers, drinking, and swearing. Edith's condition worsened daily as she contracted a brain infection. By the time they ran into Charles on the road a few miles east of Lawrence, she did not recognize her father. The Lovejoys found shelter at the home of some newly arrived New Englanders who had just lost a child of their own to the epidemic. A neighbor, Sara Robinson, noted the Lovejoy's trials in her diary the night they arrived: "The wing of the dark angel is hovering near to bear away a little child. . . . The measles have been fatal here beyond all experience." Edith died the next day, leaving Julia to write in her diary: "I am now about 6 months advanced in pregnancy and why I live is more than I can tell."[37]

After the Lovejoys settled in Manhattan, Julia, then forty-three years old, gave birth to Irving, her last child and the first child born in the town. Charles, demonstrating his consistent lack of judgment concerning the welfare of his family, returned East, leaving Julia alone again for months. On his return, Charles had to ride hundreds of miles out of his way through Iowa and Nebraska Territory because Missourians had barred the river route to all New Englanders. Julia passed her time writing letters to editors describing life on the edge of freedom's battlefield. She told stories about Satan incarnated as Southern border ruffians and related the inconveniences of frontier life: malaria, snakebite, and cornbread, a southern delicacy many New Englanders considered inedible. Julia's militant dispatches rivaled those of any man writing for the radical New York *Tribune*. "We never turned politician," she wrote, "until the wrongs of Kansas, heaped mountain-high compelled us to it." Her commitment to the anti-slavery cause became evident when the Lovejoys broke with the Methodist-Episcopal Church. Julia defined her feelings in a column: "Unless some measures are adopted at the next General Conference to rid the church of [slavery], I, an individual, though isolated and alone, cannot . . . remain."[38]

"The Lily *was the first paper published devoted to the interests of woman and so far as I know, the first one owned, edited, and published by a woman. It was a novel thing for me to do in those days and I was little fitted for it, but the force of circumstances led me into it and strength was given me to carry it through."*

Amelia Jenks Bloomer.[39]

Charles's absences allowed Julia to realize her lifelong goal of preaching the gospel. She substituted in the pulpit "with much acceptance to the people," her brother later noted. But even as she blazed new trails for women, she cautioned others to hang back. She found herself inclined to campaign for the 1856 Republican Presidential candidate, John Charles Fremont, who advocated a free Kansas, but, as she wrote for the Concord *Independent Democrat*, she would instead attend to her "sick and suffering" family. "We hate these gadders abroad—these women-lecturers who are continually at the old theme 'woman's rights,' while the poor man at home is in a sad plight . . . and his pants are all out at the knee. . . . Ladies in their own proper sphere could assist in the coming election. Let little misses and young ladies in their ornamental work for the parlor, have the names of 'Fremont and Jessie' wrought in choicest colors; let the matrons in the dairy-room, make a mammoth 'Fremont cheese' to be eaten with zest at their annual State or County Fair."[40]

Fremont lost the election, despite his popular wife Jessie Benton Fremont and any cheeses or embroidered parlor cushions. Four years later the Republicans won, but Abraham Lincoln's victory threatened the South enough that South Carolina seceded and the Kansas Troubles spread across the nation. Charles Lovejoy joined the 7th Regular Kansas Cavalry, serving as chaplain to the troops known as the Jayhawkers. Julia, then living south of Lawrence with Irving, sent dispatches describing continuing border warfare. When guerrilla warrior William Quantrill burned the town that symbolized abolitionism and murdered 185 men and boys, Julia's was one of the reports flashed to a shocked Union: "Such a day of mourning as was yesterday never dawned upon Kansas. The air was dense with the smoke of burning buildings, and the prince of darkness and his allies never devised greater schemes of cruelty, to throw back half murdered victims into the flames and roast them!"[41]

The Kansas 7th traveled to Corinth, Mississippi, in 1864, and Julia accompanied the troops for a time, teaching at two schools—one for white children and another for blacks. She sent dispatches about the hospitals and the freed slaves to religious newspapers. After the War, she and Charles followed the Methodist circuit to Illinois but soon returned to Kansas. Julia's sons both became ministers, a legacy that must have been one of the joys of her difficult, courageous life.

SAWTOOTH VARIATION,
by an unknown maker, 1840-1860
40" x 48".
Collection of Erma Kirkpatrick and
Harold McCurdy.
When is a Sawtooth block a *Kansas
Troubles*? Probably when it's set in a
four-patch pinwheel, but setting the
squares in strips of large-scale prints
also lends a Civil-War-era look.

ACTIVITY FOR RE-ENACTORS: INTERVIEW THE SOLDIERS

Julia Louisa Lovejoy and Jane Gray Swisshelm covered the Civil War, and their
presence in camp allows today's female re-enactors to assume the role of newspaper reporter. While camped with the Kansas 7th in Mississippi, Julia's letters
covered human interest stories—courage and suffering in the hospitals, joys and
confusion in new-found freedom for the slaves. The old political fires she tended
during the Kansas Troubles continued to spark stories of combat and victory.

As a newspaper correspondent, you'll need to work as hard as she did to get
your interviews. Bring graceful calling cards with your name and perhaps the
name of your newspaper to leave with the officers you want to interview. You'll
also need period paper and a pencil. Prepare a list of questions that Julia might
have asked the Union soldiers:

WOMEN AND GIRLS at General S. P.
Heintzelman's camp in Alexandria,
Virginia.

* Who were they going to vote for in the 1864 election? And why?

* How did they feel about the Emancipation Proclamation?

* When would the War be over?

* Had they seen any recent examples of gallant courage?

* Should the North accept a compromise with slavery or pursue
  unconditional surrender?

* How were their physical needs being met? Did they have enough food,
  medicine, clothing?

* What did they miss most about home?

Kansas Troubles

Kansas Troubles, machine pieced,
hand appliquéd, and machine quilted by Rosie Mayhew,
Topeka, Kansas, 1999.

Kansas Troubles is a variation of a sawtooth block quite popular in the years before the Civil War. We have no idea what the quilters called it back then; they may have had no special name. The earliest reference to the name I've found is in a catalog from a St. Louis pattern company, the Ladies Art Company, from the 1890s, when the troubles in Kansas were fairly recent memories of the Civil War.

Rosie Mayhew's version of Kansas Troubles features a border I designed to represent John Greenleaf Whittier's poem, "Song of the Kansas Immigrant." Whittier advised Kansas immigrants to plant New England pines beside the Southern cotton trees. We assume he knew that cotton didn't grow on trees. He might have been thinking of the cottonwoods that thrive near Kansas's rivers. Kansas gardeners know how hard it is to keep a New England pine tree happy in our climate, with its unpredictable drought patterns, but in this quilt, the New England pines and Kansas cottonwoods flourish side-by-side.

Size: 104" x 92"

30 Kansas Troubles blocks, 12" finished

Border, 12" finished

FABRIC REQUIREMENTS

LIGHT BLUE: $1^1/2$ yards for the blocks

DARK BLUE: 2 yards for the blocks

LIGHT COLORS: $7^1/2$ yards total for the block background and border

DARK GREEN: 4 yards for the appliqué trees, outer border, and binding

BACKING: $8^1/4$ yards

BATTING: 108" x 96"

FREEZER PAPER

CUTTING

- Cut 26 squares $12^1/2$" x $12^1/2$" from background fabrics for appliqué border.

- Cut 120 using template A (page 45) **or** 60 squares $6^7/8$" x $6^7/8$" from background fabrics, then cut in half diagonally.

- Cut 120 using template B (page 45) **or** 120 squares 2" x 2" from background fabrics.

- Cut 480 using template C (page 45) **or** 240 squares $2^3/8$" x $2^3/8$" from background fabrics, then cut in half diagonally or use the gridding method on page 118.

- Cut 720 using template C (page 45) **or** 360 squares $2^3/8$" x $2^3/8$" from dark blue, then cut in half diagonally or use the gridding method on page 118.

- Cut 120 using template D (page 45) **or** 30 squares $4^1/4$" x $4^1/4$" from light blue fabric, then cut in half diagonally.

- Cut 2 lengthwise strips $4^1/2$" x 94" for the outer side borders and 2 lengthwise strips $4^1/2$" x 106" from green for the outer top and bottom borders.

- Cut 12 squares 12" x 12" from freezer paper. On the dull side of the freezer paper, trace Cotton(wood) trees on 6 squares and Pine trees on the other 6 and cut out.

- Iron the freezer paper tree patterns (shiny side down) to the right side of the green fabric. Cut 6 Cotton(wood) trees (page 46) and 6 Pine trees (page 46), adding $1/4$" seam allowance. You will cut a total of 26 trees (13 of each), but to reuse the freezer paper you should cut more after the first trees have been appliquéd.

- Cut backing fabric into three equal lengths. Piece to create backing (page 118).

- Cut 9 strips $2^1/4$" x 42" for binding.

THE QUILT TOP

Blocks
Sawtooth Triangle Squares

1. Piece 480 squares that are half dark blue and half light blue. Press.

 =

Sawtooth triangle squares

Or try machine piecing squares of right-triangles using a mass-production method like the sawtooth grid described on page 118. You'll need to grid the fabric into $2^3/8$" squares for finished $1^1/2$" squares of light and dark triangles.

Block Assembly

1. Sew two of the small sawtooth triangle squares together. Press.

2. Add a small, dark triangle C to the right-hand side of this unit. Press.

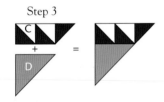

Step 1 Step 2

3. Add a triangle D. Press.

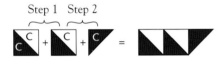

Step 3

4. Sew two more of the small sawtooth triangle squares together. Press.

5. Add a square B to the right-hand side and a small, dark triangle C to the left-hand side of this pieced unit. Press.

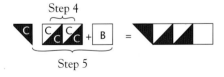

Step 4

Step 5

6. Add this pieced unit to the unit pieced in steps 1-3. Press.

7. Add a triangle A. Press.

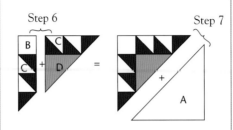

Step 6

Step 7

Make 4 per block

8. Sew the units together. Make 30 blocks.

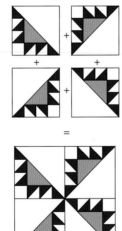

Step 8

Assembling the Quilt Top

1. Sew the blocks into rows. Press.

2. Sew the rows together. Press.

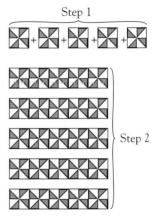

Step 1

Step 2

Borders

Appliqué Border

1. Sew five of the appliqué border squares together for the top border. Repeat for the bottom border. Press.

2. Position and pin six of the trees on the top border, referring to the quilt photograph. The seams of the border will line up with the centers of the trees. Line up the centers of the first and last trees in the row on the raw edge of the border strip. (One side of these two trees will hang off the end of the border strip.

3. Appliqué the center four trees to the top border (but not the trees that are hanging off the end of the border strip; these will be done later) using the needle-turn method, tucking the fabric under as you go (page 116). Carefully remove the freezer paper from the appliquéd trees as you go. You will reuse the freezer paper to cut more appliqué trees. Repeat for the bottom border.

4. Sew eight of the appliqué border squares together. Repeat. Press.

5. Iron seven of the freezer paper patterns (refer to the quilt photo-graph) to the right side of the green fabric. Position and pin seven of the trees on one side border, refer-ring to the quilt photograph. The seams on the border will line up with the centers of the trees. Repeat for the other side border.

6. Add the top and bottom borders to the quilt top. Press.

7. Add the side borders to the quilt top. Press.

8. Reposition the trees that have not been appliquéd yet so the seams on the border line up with the centers of the trees. Appliqué the remaining trees.

Outer Border

Add the 94" lengths to the sides and the 106" lengths to the top and bottom of the quilt top. Press.

Quilting

1. Layer and baste the quilt (page 119).

2. Our Kansas Troubles quilts (pages 38 and 42) are machine-quilted. Whether hand quilting or machine quilting, you will probably want to outline the trees and do a utility quilting pattern across the blocks. Diagonal lines or a grid would be good.

3. Bind the quilt (page 119).

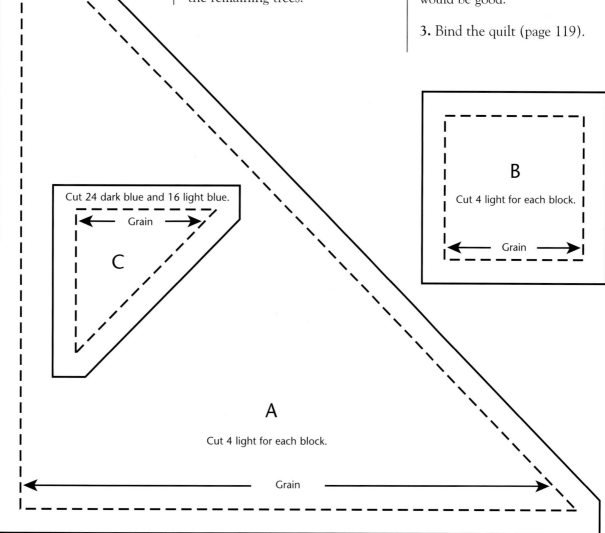

Cut 24 dark blue and 16 light blue.

Grain

C

B

Cut 4 light for each block.

Grain

A

Cut 4 light for each block.

Grain

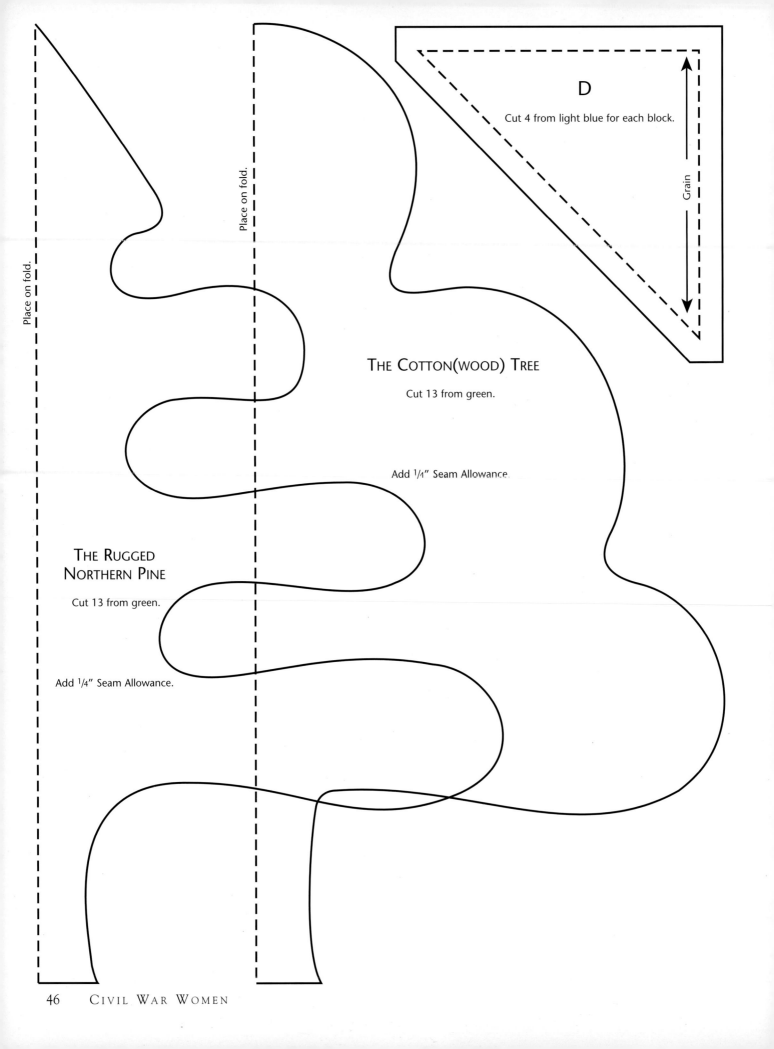

Place on fold.

Place on fold.

D

Cut 4 from light blue for each block.

Grain

THE COTTON(WOOD) TREE

Cut 13 from green.

Add 1/4" Seam Allowance.

THE RUGGED
NORTHERN PINE

Cut 13 from green.

Add 1/4" Seam Allowance.

CHAPTER 4

REMEMBERING BURSHEBA FRISTOE YOUNGER AND OTHER REFUGEES

October 17, 1862, Gray Summit, Missouri

"My dear Husband: We were visited last night about two o'clock by the bushwhackers. I was up with the baby when they came. . . . They got both of the guns and then went up stair, took some of my bed blankets, three pair of coarse sox. . . . They then searched the bureau drawers. They even took as small a thing as comb and brush. They then came down called for whiskey and said they had been told there was some in the house and they intended to have it."

Permelia Hardeman[43]

Permelia Hardeman, like so many Missouri women, suffered greatly during the Civil War. She lost her quilts and blankets, clothing, and other household items to rampant thievery cloaked in Union and Confederate patriotism. Permelia left her tale in her letters, but she is unusual in Missouri, where few women's words written during the War have been published. Bursheba Younger, who left nothing but her children to tell her story, surely lived one of the most woeful tales of the War. The Border War took her husband, her homes, and her health. She was left only one legacy—the reputation as mother to an outlaw clan.

Bursheba Younger (1816-1870) might have had a quilt much like the Crown of Thorns. The pattern was popular in Tennessee in the 1840s and '50s and in places settled by immigrants from Tennessee, including Texas and Missouri. The Biblical name Crown of Thorns symbolizes Bursheba's trials in the midst of the worst guerrilla warfare ever to take place in the United States. If she had such an elegant quilt, it was surely lost to her by War's end. What was not stolen was burned, and what was not burned was abandoned when Bursheba and her neighbors were banished from their homes.

Bursheba lived in Western Missouri, a stronghold of Southern sentiment in a Union state. Missouri had been settled by Southern immigrants, like her Tennessee family, who in one generation established a near replica of the deep south. Declaration of Civil War legitimized a seven-year-old border war in which Missourians and Kansas settlers had battled for the soul of the Kansas territory. Americans opposed to further extension of slavery into the west staked claims in Kansas, alarming Missourians, who feared losing slaves and a way of life. Jayhawkers from Kansas and Bushwhackers from Missouri criss-crossed borders to terrorize partisans and innocent bystanders alike.

HARPER'S WEEKLY portrayed civilian assaults by Confederate guerrillas.

When the deep south seceded in early 1861, Missouri's governor tried following the same path. The Union Army foiled him, declaring martial law and driving his Confederate government into hiding in the countryside. Never a star on the Confederate flag, Missouri was doomed to suffer more battles than any state but Virginia and Tennessee. Most skirmishes pitted Missourian against Missourian as Union armies fought Confederate. Soldiers killed soldiers, but soldiers also fought civilians; civilians murdered each other and vigilantes terrorized the population in an ever-escalating game of revenge.

In 1830, when Bursheba Leighton Fristoe married Henry Washington Younger, both families were successful Missouri pioneers, living the Southern way of life on the Western frontier. Bursheba probably knew that her new husband's father kept three families. With Sarah (Henry's mother), his second wife, he'd produced six children. With Permelia Wilson, a neighbor and possibly one of his slaves, he'd fathered nine illegitimate children, and with a slave in his house, Elizabeth Simpson, he had two children. At the time such black and white liaisons were often discussed, as Mary Chesnut wrote in 1861: "Like the patriarchs of old our men live all in one house with their wives and their concubines, and the mulattos one sees in every family exactly resemble the white children—and every lady tells you who is the father of all the mulatto children in everybody's household, but those in her own she seems to think drop from the clouds, or pretends to think so."[44]

Henry became a better husband than his father, providing Bursheba with a stable and prosperous life. When the War broke out he owned businesses, farms, slaves, and city and country homes in both Cass and Jackson Counties. Bursheba gave birth to nine daughters and five sons, a baby every other year for nearly 30 years. Most of the Younger's girls had married by 1861, but their sons, Thomas, Coleman, James, Robert, and John, and the two youngest daughters lived at home. Both Youngers and Fristoes enjoyed extended families with strong ties. Bursheba's sisters, her mother Polly, and her brother lived nearby. Among the family members close to Bursheba was her slave Suse, who was purchased in 1850 when Suse was about fourteen years old. Like most Missouri slaveholders, the Youngers owned fewer than ten.

During the difficult years of 1854 to 1856, Henry promoted slavery in Kansas, riding from Cass County, Missouri, to Louisiana, Kansas, a new town he had founded in Douglas County. He voted in the Kansas territorial elections and served as a representative in the first Territorial Legislature, the so-called "Bogus Legislature" hated by legitimate Kansas settlers because of its pro-slavery stance and non-resident members.

By the beginning of the Civil War, Missouri goals for Kansas slavery had failed and Henry Younger was home tending to his family, farms, businesses, and a government mail route. His politics were similar to those of his neighbors. Most Missourians opposed Secession and hoped to ride out the war as neutrals. But neutrality soon became an untenable position in western Missouri. War encouraged border residents to settle old scores and war created new antagonisms between Union and Confederate sympathizers. The country was devastated by the hatred. Traveling on the Missouri River, Kansan Julia Lovejoy wrote: "Business is all stagnated throughout the State—fine farms deserted, and the sad effects of war seen on every hand. . . . Secesh is dead in Missouri though deadly hatred to the United States is concealed in many bosoms, and this hatred breaks out in murder and horse-stealing and robbing Union men at every opportunity."[46]

REBEL REFUGEES in camp, from the *Illustrated London News.*

Kansans in Union uniforms rode into Missouri under the banners of the newly legitimate Jayhawker regiments. Henry Younger may have been a Jayhawker target from the outset of the War. Anyone looking for enemies of Kansas's Free-State cause need only check the list of pro-slavery representatives to that first "Bogus Legislature." In July, 1862, a Kansas cavalryman came across a body near the Shawnee Indian Mission on the state line. Lying dead in the road was a "finely-formed, well-built, handsome man, dressed in a suit of the finest texture, betokening the man of wealth and standing in the community." Searching the body, the soldiers found a large packet of cash and information that the murdered man was Henry Younger of Harrisonville, Missouri. They contacted Bursheba, who sent a family member to bring Henry home. The Kansans also returned the money Henry had been carrying, a kindness rarely recorded in those years on the border.[47]

Why was Henry Younger shot? His sons blamed a vicious Missourian in the Union army, who carried a grudge over an insult at a dance. Others called it random highway robbery, although Henry's cash remained on his body. Such stories may have covered political murder as Kansas Jayhawkers took revenge on an old pro-slave enemy. Or Henry may have been punished for his son's crimes. Like so many of his friends and kin, Thomas Coleman Younger, known as Bud or Cole, chose a guerrilla's life as his way to fight the war. Cole later told people he made a vow of vengeance over the body of his father, but the cause and effect in the death of Henry Younger is unclear. Did Cole turn killer to avenge his father's murder or did Henry die as a lesson to his neighbors who permitted their sons to live in the bush and attack Yankee soldiers at will?

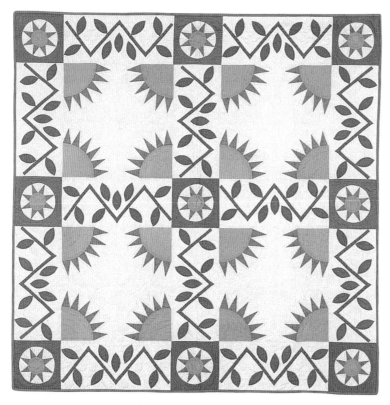

CROWN OF THORNS OR ROCKY MOUNTAIN, machine pieced, hand appliquéd, and hand quilted by Rosie Mayhew, Topeka, Kansas, 1999. Rosie's quilt in 19th-century colors is an adaptation of a pattern found in Tennessee. Instead of spiky pieced sashing, these Tennessee variations feature appliquéd vines.

Bursheba was left with an impressive inheritance, three boys and two girls at home, and considerable grief. Son Jim joined his brother Cole in the bush with William Quantrill, Bloody Bill Anderson and other notorious Bushwhackers. Henry's estate, caught in a web of martial law since Missouri had no official justice system during the War, soon amounted to nothing. Federal troops and Unionist vigilantes continued to punish Bursheba, stealing Henry's large stable of horses and burning her house and those of her sister and her mother. The family recalled that when the troops threatened to torch her house, Bursheba begged them to spare it to shelter a sick daughter. They taunted her with one more night on the condition that she light the fire herself in the morning. She kept her end of the bargain, and watched the house burn as she and four children and Suse stood in the snow.

Throughout her tribulations, as she moved from relative's house to relative's house, Bursheba probably aided the guerrillas who were hiding in the woods and caves along the Little Blue and Sni Rivers.

A little over a year after Henry's death, Federal officials arrested a group of women and girls who were known to aid and abet the fugitives, sisters, and cousins of the bushwhackers. Bursheba probably knew many of them as neighbors and kin. When the jail building collapsed, five Missouri women died under the rock walls, enraging the guerrillas to new fury. Cole and Jim Younger were among the 400 Missourians who raided the Free-State symbol, Lawrence, Kansas, at dawn in August, 1863. In two or three wild hours, the Missourians murdered 185 men and boys. The Federal government, shocked by this climax to a decade of revenge killings, issued Order Number 11, banishing Missourians from four counties along the Kansas line. Bursheba, her family, and friends took what stock and possessions they had remaining and walked south to Scyene, Texas, near Sherman.

Bursheba, Suse, and several children returned to Jackson County in 1870. Her three sons refused to live within the law after Appomatox. With their neighbors, the James brothers, they robbed banks throughout the midwest, defining American outlaw mythology. Bursheba suffered a final heartache when a mob, looking for Cole and Bob, tried a trick they had learned during the war. Demanding that Bursheba's youngest son John talk about his bankrobbing brothers, the mob hung him, then cut him down just in time to save his life. The family believed this one last act of terrorism caused Bursheba's death on her 54th birthday.

ACTIVITY FOR RE-ENACTORS: MAKE A TOBACCO BAG FOR A SOLDIER

Sewing small gifts for the soldiers is an excellent camp activity for female re-enactors. Along with photographs and sweetheart flags, soldiers carried handmade tobacco bags as evidence of a girl back home. Southerner Kate Stone wrote in her diary of making tobacco bags for young men, noting at the end of 1862 that "our scraps of silk and velvet and embroidery silk are nearly exhausted." Kate's elegant bags were part of her flirtations with the soldiers she met. In 1865, she sewed a black velvet bag embroidered with scarlet fuchsias for her future husband.[51]

Confederate nurse Kate Cumming made bags of more serviceable cloth for her patients. "I hinted to some of the ladies about having tobacco bags made, as the tobacco gets scattered all over the beds, but none offered to make them. Some were kind enough to give me the pieces to have them made. After the labors of the day are past, Miss Womack and myself make as many as we can."[52]

A Confederate memoirist remembered her husband returning so shabby that she did not recognize him. "He was without socks and his ankles showed naked and sore between trousers and shoes. He had on a bedticking shirt, a tobacco-bag of bedticking hung by a string from a button of his shirt."[53]

Tobacco bags, whether silk or homespun, were often embroidered or appliquéd. Stars, hearts, or flags personalized a soldier's gift. If your soldier doesn't smoke, the bag could hold small treasures.

To make a tobacco bag cut a 5" by 7" rectangle of fabric such as plaid flannel or coarse, plain cotton. The Confederate rebus, "My [heart] is true to Dixie," was cross-stitched on the original. Or ink a Union star. Decorate the bag before you assemble it. Fold the bag in half and sew a seam on the side and bottom. Turn the top edge inside about 1" and sew a channel for the cord. Cut 7" of cord or string. Make two holes for the cord and thread it through the channel, knotting the ends so they don't slip through. You can finish the openings for the cord with a nice buttonhole stitch, but the old bags I've seen have raw edges there.

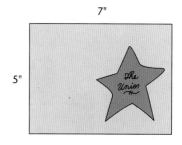

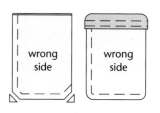

Tobacco Bag

Doggy Mountain

Doggy Mountain (Rocky Mountain), machine pieced and machine quilted by Mary Fischer Boyd,
Daly City, California, 1999.
Mary used every brown scrap in her collection, a reason for the name
"Doggy Mountain." Many of her old brown scraps were real dogs on their
own, but, when combined, the whole is far more attractive than the parts.

We can imagine Bursheba obtaining quilt patterns from her mother's relatives back in McMinnville, Tennessee. One might have been a design we call "New York Beauty," a name considered a ridiculous Yankee-ism in the South, where it's "Rocky Mountain" or "Crown of Thorns." The design may represent the Rocky Mountains that attracted so many pioneers during the Civil War era. One was Elizabeth Dixon Smith, who wrote in her diary, "August 1, 1848. Passed over the Rocky mountain, the backbone of America. It is all rocks on top and they are split into pieces and turned up edgeways. Oh, that I had time and talent to describe this curious country."

One quilt uncovered by the Missouri Heritage Quilt Project had a note pinned to it with the names "Road to the White House" and "Poke (Polk) and Dallas." Tennessee was proud of favorite son James K. Polk, who ran for President in 1844 with George Dallas. The Democrats advocated statehood for Texas, a controversial position because Texas would be a slave state. Polk and many Tennesseans favored slavery's extension into the new western territories as far as the Rocky Mountains. Did the Rocky Mountain design symbolize Polk's 1844 campaign and the continuing free-state/slave-state controversy that eventually resulted in the Civil War? Were the many post-war examples secret evidence of unreconstructed Southern sympathies?

Bursheba Younger has hundreds of descendants. One may own a quilt she pieced, but until we find one, "Crown of Thorns" is a good remembrance of her life.

Size: 53" x 53"

Sixteen fan blocks, 8" x 8" finished

Nine sunflower blocks, 7" x 7" finished

Sashing strips, 7" x 16" finished

FABRIC REQUIREMENTS

OFF-WHITE: $2^3/4$ yards for background and binding

BROWN SCRAPS: 3 yards total for triangles and sunflowers

YELLOW/GOLD SCRAPS: $1/2$ yard total for sunflowers

RED SCRAPS: $1/4$ yard total for sunflowers

BACKING: $3^1/4$ yards

BATTING: 57" x 57"

CUTTING

- Cut 12 strips $1^1/2$" x $16^1/2$" from off-white fabric for sashing.

- Cut 16 using template B (page 58) from off-white fabric.

- Cut 16 using template C (page 59) from off-white fabric.

- Cut 9 using template E (page 58) from red fabrics.

- Cut 36 using template F (page 58) from off-white fabric.

- Cut the backing fabric into two equal lengths. Piece to create backing (page 118).

- Cut 5 strips $2^1/4$" x 42" for binding.

THE QUILT TOP

Fan Blocks
The fan blocks will be machine pieced over the paper foundations given. This new technique makes the fans and spiky points manageable. (How did they do it by hand in 1850?) You'll need sixteen fan blocks (8" x 8" finished).

1. Make 16 copies of the fan block arc—template A (page 57).

Position the fabrics on the blank side of the paper and stitch on the printed side of the paper.

2. Begin with a rectangular piece of off-white fabric larger than the first triangle on the paper pattern. Hold the pattern and fabric up to the light and position the fabric right side up so it completely covers the triangle and extends at least $1/4$" beyond the printed lines. Pin it in place.

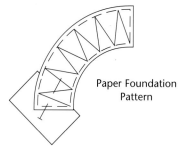

Paper Foundation Pattern

Position first fabric.

3. Cut a rectangular piece of dark fabric larger than the next triangle on the paper pattern. Place it wrong side up on top of the first fabric.

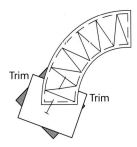

Position second fabric.

4. Hold the pattern up to the light and open the dark fabric on what will be the seam line to make sure that it will completely cover the triangle after the seam is sewn.

5. Stitch exactly on the line. Trim the seam allowance to $^1/_4$".

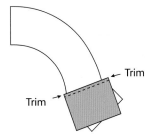

Stitch on line and trim to $^1/_4$" seam allowance.

6. Open the dark piece of fabric so it is right side up, and press with your iron or finger press.

7. Continue adding triangles, alternating the off-white and dark fabrics, until you have covered the entire arc. Trim around the outside edge of the paper patttern.

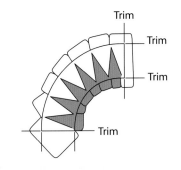

Finish piecing the arc and trim.

8. Pin and stitch pieces B and C to the pieced arc to complete the block. Press. Make 16. Remove the paper pattern.

9. Sew four fan blocks together, following the quilt photograph. Press. Make 4.

Sunflower Blocks for the Sashing
You'll need nine sunflower blocks (7" finished). Machine piecing on paper makes these easy. Each arc is half a sunflower.

1. Make 18 copies of the sunflower block arc—template D (page 59).

2. Follow the instructions in Steps 2 through 7 above to piece the arcs.

3. Stitch two arcs together to form a circle. Press.

4. Pin and stitch piece E in the center. Press. Make 9.

5. Stitch four of piece F to form a circle in the center. Press.

6. Pin and stitch the sunflower circle to the center of the F pieces to complete the block. Press. Make 9. Remove the paper pattern.

Sashing
1. Make 48 copies of template G (page 57). Tape pairs of patterns together, end-to-end, matching a dotted line to a dashed line, to create 24 strips 16" long.

2. Follow the instructions in Steps 2 through 7 in Fan Blocks above. Make 24.

3. Sew the pieced strips made above to the $1^1/_2$" strips of background fabric. Remove the paper pattern.

Assembling the Quilt Top
1. Lay out the fan blocks, sunflower blocks, and sashing strips, referring to the quilt photograph.

2. Sew the sashing and blocks in rows. Sew the rows together.

QUILTING

1. Layer and baste the quilt (page 119).

2. Mary machine quilted in an all-over meander and outlined each triangle. She quilted a star where the fan blocks meet.

3. Bind the quilt (page 119).

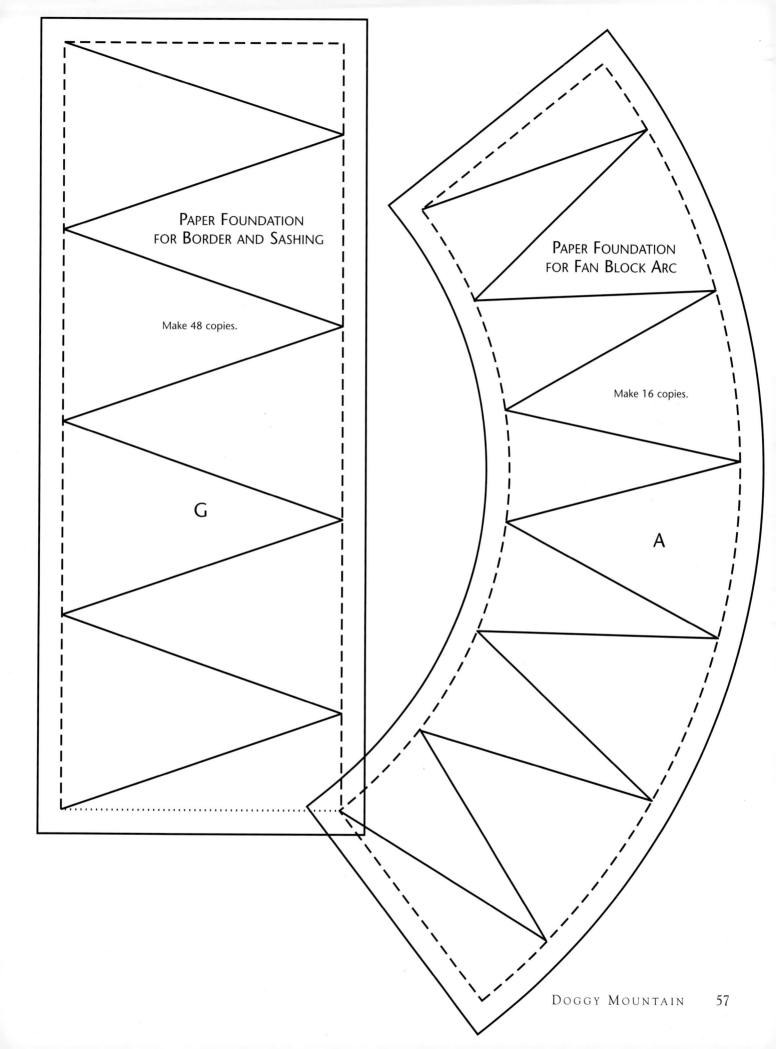

PAPER FOUNDATION
FOR BORDER AND SASHING

Make 48 copies.

G

PAPER FOUNDATION
FOR FAN BLOCK ARC

Make 16 copies.

A

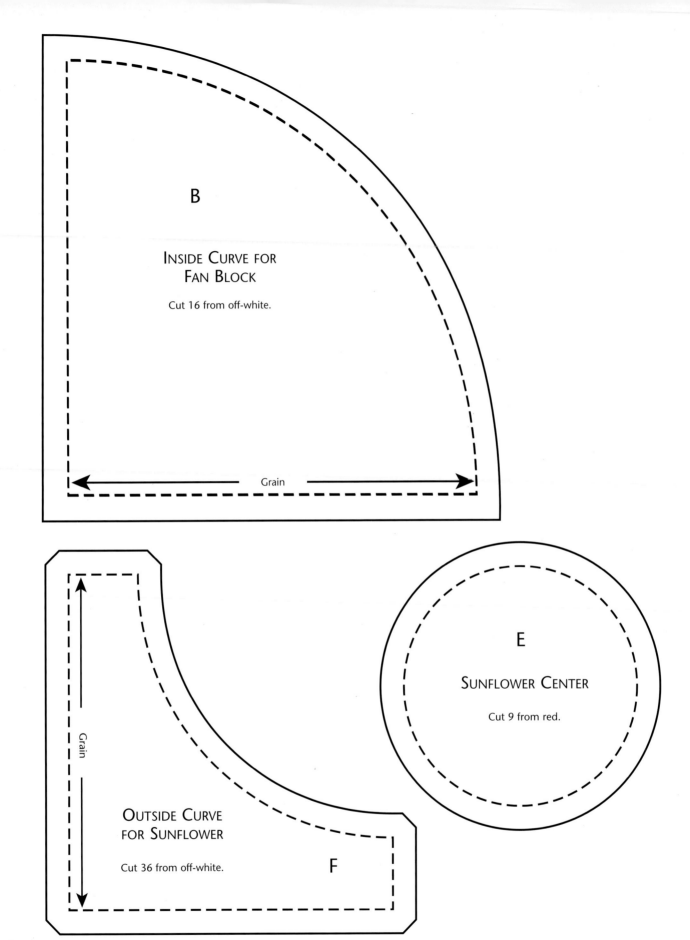

B

INSIDE CURVE FOR
FAN BLOCK

Cut 16 from off-white.

Grain

Grain

OUTSIDE CURVE
FOR SUNFLOWER

Cut 36 from off-white.

F

E

SUNFLOWER CENTER

Cut 9 from red.

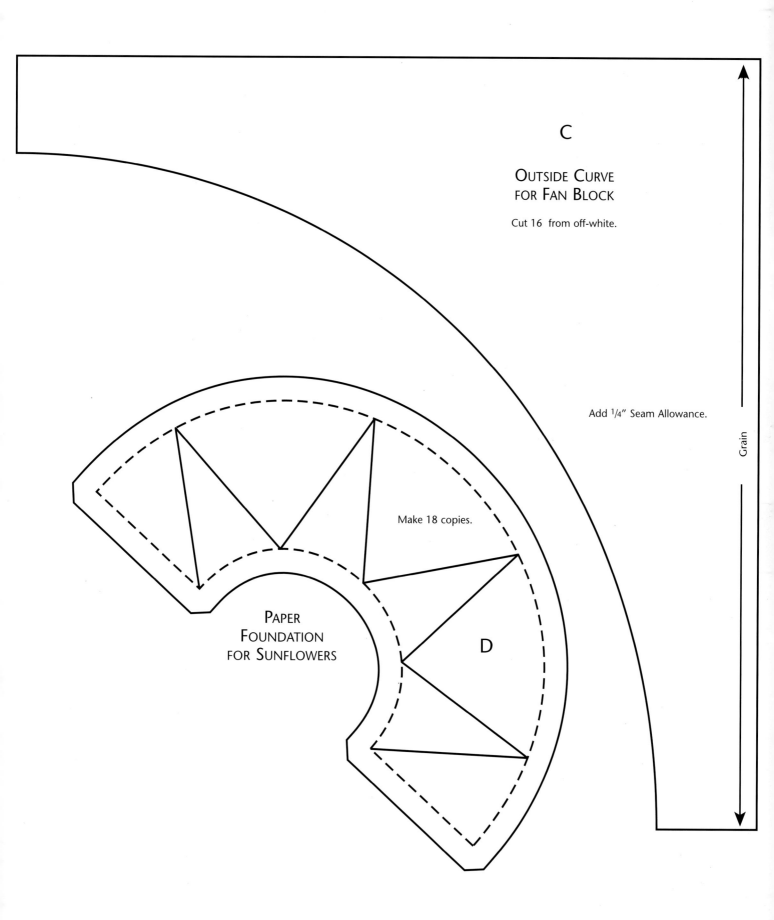

C

OUTSIDE CURVE FOR FAN BLOCK

Cut 16 from off-white.

Add 1/4" Seam Allowance.

Make 18 copies.

PAPER FOUNDATION FOR SUNFLOWERS

D

Grain

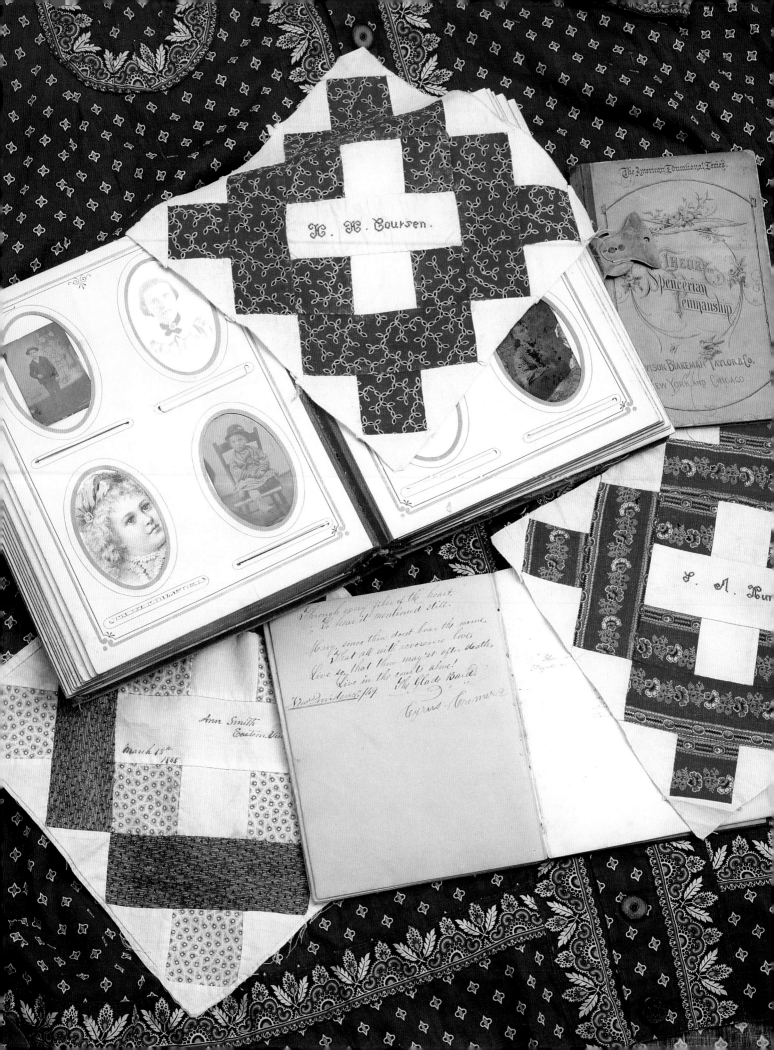

CHAPTER 5

REMEMBERING HANNAH ROPES AND OTHER NURSES

"We had in our tents two fathers, with their wounded sons, and a nice old German mother with her boy. She had come in from Wisconsin, and brought with her a patchwork bed-quilt for her son, thinking he might have lost his blanket; and there he laid all covered up in his quilt, looking so homelike and feeling so, too, no doubt, with his good old mother close at his side."[54]

When the Civil War began, Hannah Ropes (1809-1863) helped to define a new career for women: the professional nurse. We can imagine her stitching a quilt by candlelight in the Union Hotel Hospital in Georgetown in the District of Columbia, as she sat by a dozing soldier's bed, ready to reach out and hold his hand if he started from a fitful dream. Born in Maine in 1809 into a family of lawyers and politicians, Hannah grew to be an independent young woman with an interest in reform and non-traditional religion. She married William Ropes when she was twenty-four years old and converted to the Swedenborgian faith a few years later. William was a teacher and principal in Waltham, Massachusetts, near Boston. There Hannah became involved in anti-slavery activities, making the acquaintance of free-soil activists like Massachusetts's Senator Charles Sumner. She raised four children and lost two. Sometime around Hannah's 40th birthday, her husband left for Florida, leaving her a single woman. There are no divorce records and no record that she ever saw or heard from him again.[55]

In 1855, Hannah and fourteen-year-old Alice followed Hannah's son Ned on the crusade to make the new territory of Kansas a free state. Quilts were a part of Hannah Ropes's life. When she unpacked her trunks in far-off Kansas in 1855, she found comfort in her family quilts. "Two quilts of stripped-up dresses, done by your hand, dear mother, are brought from the chest, and with them sheets, too, with the New England clean-odor still in their folds! What nice little beds they seem, if they are but prairie grass."[56]

They spent six months, a fever-ridden fall and harsh winter, in Lawrence. Ned's cabin became a makeshift hospital where Hannah cared for typhoid and malaria victims. Soon, she too contracted malaria from the mosquitoes thriving near the Kansas River, and she and Alice returned to Massachusetts. She shaped her frontier experiences into a book, *Six Months in Kansas By A Lady*, which became another spark that kept alive the anti-slavery flames during the years of the Kansas Troubles.

Opposite page

AUTOGRAPH AND PHOTOGRAPH ALBUMS reminded Victorians of friends separated by distance or death. In the 1820s, bound album books became a fad, as women perfected a verse and a signature. By the 1840s, the fashion was extended to album or friendship quilts, on which signatures were inked or cross stitched.

After Fort Sumter, Hannah answered the call for women volunteers to work with the wounded and ill. Despite disapproval from female society and male doctors who believed women did not belong in hospitals, Hannah found a useful place. Secretary of War Simon Cameron appointed social reformer Dorothea Dix to organize a corps of nurses. Dix had earned a national reputation for her work with the mentally ill. Using a military model, she enlisted nurses and provided training, discipline, and supervision. Nurses were paid the same salary as privates by the War Department. Dix's dictatorial manner and deference to the Army surgeons made her as unpopular with the women who worked for her as with the men who supervised her. Letters, memoirs, and diaries often ridiculed her. George Templeton Strong of the Sanitary Commission described her as a "philanthropic lunatic," and journalist Jane Swisshelm called her "a self sealing can of horror tied up with red tape."[57]

Her "Plan for Nurses" dictated the rules:

"No women under thirty need apply to serve in government hospitals. All nurses are required to be plain-looking women. Their dresses must be brown or black with no bows, no curls, no jewelry and no hoop skirts. No young ladies should be sent at all but women who can afford to give their services and time and meet part of the expenses or the whole. . . . sober, earnest, self-sacrificing, self-sustained, calm, gentle, quite active and steadfast and willing to take and to execute the directions of the surgeons."[58]

Hannah Ropes possessed all the traits but the last, which meant she continually battled the surgeons with a different idea of a nurse's duties. Despite her strong-mindedness, Hannah rose to a supervisory role, overseeing the hospital routine.

SARAH JANE FULL HILL remembered that on her hospital ship, "We all wore black dresses with large white aprons while on duty, and that was most of the time." But it's doubtful these pretty young girls in their outrageous hats were real nurses. The photo was sold at New York's Sanitary Commission Fair. Georgeanna Woolsey wrote her sister after her training that she had made up "some sort of a hospital costume. . . . I have two gray cottonish cross-grained skirts, and a Zouave jacket giving free motion to the arms—so the skirts can be, one of them, always in the wash; and a white Zouave will take the place of the waist when that is in the tub. Four white aprons with waists and large pockets; two stick-out and washable petticoats to take the place of a hoop, and a nice long flannel dressing gown, which one may put on in a hurry and fly out in, if the city is bombarded or 'anything else.' " Louisa May Alcott wore a red *rigolette* or scarf around her head, a look that wouldn't have appealed to Confederate Quaker Cornelia Hancock, who patched together a uniform during the embargo. "We have always made a rule of wearing the simplest kind of dress, as we think any other kind sadly out of place in a hospital; calico or homespun is the only dress fit to wear, but to get the former is a rare treat."[60]

Nurse Sophronia E. Bucklin described the nurses' tasks:

"Our duties here were to distribute food to the patients, when brought up from the kitchen; wash the faces and hands, and comb the heads of the wounded; see that their bedding and clothing was kept clean and whole, bring pocket hand-kerchiefs, prepare and give the various drinks and stimulants at times as they were ordered by the surgeons."[61]

Sophronia omits mention of the nurturing necessary to comfort the soldiers, something Hannah describes well in her letters from the Georgetown hospital. "I stopped to listen to one of the night nurses; she says 'I want to speak to you about the man with the bad foot in the dining room. He could not go to sleep last night and was dreadful fussy.' 'Well,' I said, 'you should have sat down by him and held his hand awhile—it is not easy to go to sleep with so many in the room.' "[62]

A PORTRAIT of Mary Morris Husband in her nurse's uniform.

Many of the nurses' letters and diaries gloss over the sheer horror of hospital work. They daily dealt with maggots; gangrene; lockjaw; gaping, unhealing wounds; and terrified, hysterical, and demented patients. Medical knowledge was woefully ignorant; doctors had no idea that disease was germ-borne and that malaria and yellow fever were the deadly result of mosquito bites. Medical technology of the day dictated wrong-headed practices such as blistering, bleeding, and packing wounds with lint. Nursing was mainly a matter of providing comfort and wishing for luck.

Surgeons, aware of their limitations, were frustrated by their failures. Many maintained a small sense of control by bullying the women and enforcing petty regulations of the kind that confined Sophronia Bucklin, who lamented, "Women nurses were not allowed to go into the kitchen for articles of any kind." Issues between surgeons and nurses included ideas of army discipline versus common sense, as well as the conflict of private philanthropy versus government issue. Georgeanna Woolsey stood up to both Dorothea Dix and her supervising surgeon after committing the offense of fanning a dying man. "We have had an encounter with Miss Dix," she wrote her family, "that is rather the way to express it. Splendid as her career has been, she would succeed better with more graciousness of manner. However, we brought her to terms, and shall get along better." Georgy believed the doctors' rules were coolly calculated to destroy the new system. "No one knows . . . how much opposition, how much ill-will, how much unfeeling want of thought, these women nurses endured. Hardly a surgeon of whom I can think, received or treated them with even common courtesy. Government had decided that women should be employed and the army surgeons . . . determined to make their lives so unbearable that they should be forced in self-defence to leave." Cornelia Hancock summarized the age old conflict. "I ask but one thing from any surgeon, and that is, to be treated with the same respect due to men in their own sphere of life."[64]

"Number 41 ought to have soda-water and egg beaten in wine every day—Eastman, near the door; be good to him and to D. and C. and M., and read the Pickwick Papers to the poor fellow who blew himself up with gunpowder."

A note from Sarah Woolsey to her cousin Georgy, who was taking over her ward.[63]

Viewing the hospital conflicts only as men versus women or army versus civilians ignores a common problem that few women complained about in print. Their sister nurses too often indulged in improper behavior, ranging from the flirting disdained by Miss Dix to patient abuse and theft. "I have no doubt that most people think I came into the army to get a husband. . . . There are many good-looking women here who galavant around in the evening, and have a good time. I do not trouble myself much with the common herd," wrote Cornelia Hancock. Kate Cumming was also disgusted. "There is always a black sheep in every flock. . . . I was not a little astonished to hear a very pretty widow say that she never enjoyed herself so much as she had since she had been there. . . . she was told that she must try to catch a beau—and she had succeeded." Louisa May Alcott described worse sins, complaining of "the sanctified nurse who sung hymns and prayed violently while stealing the men's watches and money" and of con artists who were attentive until "the patients had made their wills in her favor."[65]

But the worst enemy was disease. Far more soldiers died of infection than from
battlefield injuries. The same diseases infected their nurses, who literally risked
their lives in their work. In late 1862, a typhoid epidemic ravaged the staff at
the Washington hospital where Louisa May Alcott and Hannah Ropes worked.
Louisa survived, just barely, to return home to Massachusetts with a bald head
and permanent frail health due to the trauma. She also carried a determination
to turn her few months of nursing into a book that became *Hospital Sketches*,
her first literary success. But the Matron, as she referred to Hannah Ropes in
the book, was not as lucky. Alice Ropes rushed to the hospital to care for her
mother after a call from Miss Dix, but Hannah failed quickly. Typhoid, which
killed many a common soldier, as well as distinguished figures such as England's
Prince Albert and Democratic Presidential candidate Stephen A. Douglas, also
killed Hannah Ropes. She left her hospital diary, the book her children published as *Civil War Nurse*.

Activity for Re-Enactors: Collect Signatures for an Album Quilt

Oak Leaf and Reel Friendship Album, made in Medford, New Jersey, by members of the Hoopes and Eachus families, inscribed 1844. Collection of Joyce Gross. Photo by Jerry DeFelice.

HICKCOX'S STENCIL CHEST
CONTAINS A COMPLETE OUTFIT FOR CUTTING
Marking Plates.

T. N. Hickcox of New York advertised in an 1862 issue of *Harper's Weekly* that he sold kits for cutting metal stencils for "Clothing, Cards, Books, &c." With Mr. Hickcox's kit of tools and one hundred brass plates, one could go into business cutting custom-made plates with names, figures, borders, and scrolls. Many of the signatures on old album quilts were inked using these handmade brass stencil plates.

An album quilt is a perfect way to record friendships and experiences. Album blocks were sometimes called "Beggar's Blocks" because one asked friends for souvenirs of their dresses as well as a signature. Bring finished blocks to camps and events and ask soldiers, officers, and civilians to sign them. You might want to bring self-addressed stamped envelopes with you to re-enactments and ask each lady to mail you a 7" x 14" piece of her dress fabric with a signed square so you can make the album blocks given in the pattern (page 70).

Making an imaginary album quilt is a great exercise in historical research. Mary Madden and I spent some time making a list of the women we wanted to honor for Mary's *Free-State Album Quilt*. We spent a longer time finding the first names of women who were generally known as Mrs. George W. Brown or the Widow Blanton. We learned a good deal about our state's Civil War history.

Other ideas for albums abound. Quilters could honor those who worked in the Underground Railroad, their own family ancestors, or nurses who labored in Union hospitals. A friend of mine is making an album saluting the women whose husbands were killed in Quantrill's Raid on Lawrence, Kansas, in 1863. And I've been photocopying the signature facsimiles sometimes found in the front of books of women's journals. Someday I want to make an album quilt "signed" by my favorite Civil War era diarists and letter writers.

Free-State Album

Free-State Album, machine pieced, hand quilted by Mary Wilk Madden,
Topeka, Kansas, 1996.
Mary's album quilt is inked with names of men and women who worked to
make the Kansas Territory a free state in the 1850s. She used a good variety
of reproduction prints.

An album quilt like Mary's is the kind of quilt Hannah Ropes might have made. During the War, women working for Soldiers' Aid Societies and the Sanitary Commission made similar quilts for soldiers in hospitals. The pattern was popular in New England from 1840 through the 1870s. *Godey's Lady's Book* published the design in 1859 but gave no name. The best name for the design might be the generic "Album Quilt," because the design usually featured inked signatures and sentiments, just like a bound autograph album book. During and shortly after the Civil War, a group of women in Canandaigua, New York, made a series of quilts in this pattern, which they called "Friendship Quilt," "Album Quilt," and "Double Tie." On the blocks they inked images of Union patriotism as well as comments about their friendship and the marriages the quilts commemorated.[67]

Size: 78" x 88"

Fifty-six blocks, 9" x 9" finished

Sashing strips and border, 1³/4" finished

FABRIC REQUIREMENTS

WHITE OR ECRU: ¹/2 yard for block centers

LIGHT-COLORED REPRODUCTION FABRICS: 10 different fat quarters (2¹/2 yards total) for the blocks

DARK-COLORED REPRODUCTION FABRICS: 12 different fat quarters (2¹/2 yards total) for the blocks

DULL PURPLE CALICO: 3 yards for sashing, border, and binding

BACKING: 5 yards

BATTING: 82" x 92"

Pigma Micron® or Gelly Roll® pen by Sakura

Freezer paper

"Accept our valued friendship,
And roll it up in cotton
And think it not illusion
Because so easily gotten."
Inscription on an album quilt.

"I wish I were a man! I would be free to do my little all, and I think I could beat some of those old fogies in dressing wounds, if not in sawing off limbs."
Letter from Jane Newton Woolsey.

CUTTING

Long sashing, border, and binding strips are cut on the lengthwise grain to avoid piecing them.

You can also use some of the sashing/border fabric in the blocks.

- Cut 224 using template A (page 70) **or** 56 squares 7¹/2" x 7¹/2" from light prints for the blocks, then cut in half diagonally twice.

- Cut 224 using template B (page 70) from dark prints, for the blocks.

- Cut 56 using template C (page 70) **or** 56 squares 2¹/2" x 2¹/2" of white or ecru for the block centers.

- Cut 8 lengthwise strips 2¹/4" x 88¹/2" from dull purple for the vertical sashing and side borders.

- Cut 2 lengthwise strips 2¹/4" x 78¹/2" from dull purple for the top and bottom borders.

- Cut 2 lengthwise strips 2¹/4" x 90" and 2 lengthwise strips 2¹/4" x 80" from dull purple for binding.

- Cut 49 strips 9¹/2" x 2¹/4" from dull purple for the horizontal sashing.

- Cut the backing fabric into two equal lengths. Piece to create backing (page 118).

INKING

It's best to ink the white centers (page 69) before you make the blocks. You can then discard any misspellings or blotches. Remember, though, there are lots of blotches on 19th-century albums, and these people, who practiced variable rather than fixed spelling, wouldn't have been too upset if they left the "i" out of "marriage." To stabilize the fabric while you are writing, iron a piece of freezer paper to the back, and remove it once it's inked. Use a permanent black pen. Pigma and Gelly Roll pens by Sakura are reliable and easy to write with.

The Quilt Top

Album Blocks

Album block

1. Piece each block as three diagonal sections. Stitch the pieces together as shown. Press.

2. Join the sections. Press.

Assembling the Quilt Top

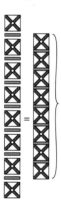

make 7 strips

1. Connect the blocks with the short sashing strips into vertical units of eight blocks each. Press.

Quilt Construction

2. Join the rows with the vertical strips of sashing between. Press.

3. Add the top and bottom borders. Press. Add the side borders. Press.

Quilting

1. Layer and baste (page 119).

2. Mary had the top hand quilted in a simple outline design, the kind of quilting typical of the 20th century. She outlined each piece, including the sashing and borders, $1/4$" from the seams. If you would rather quilt in a more typical 19th-century pattern, try a variation of diagonal lines, as shown in the diagram.

3. Bind the quilt (page 119).

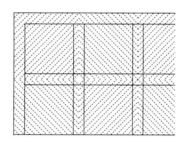

Possible quilting design

Inking Patterns

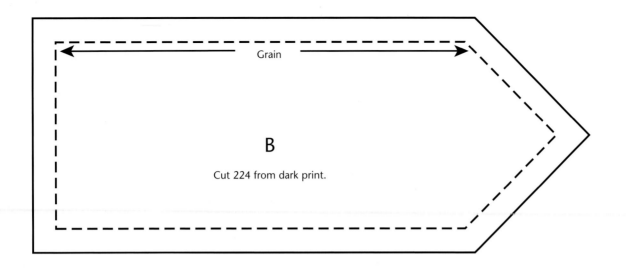

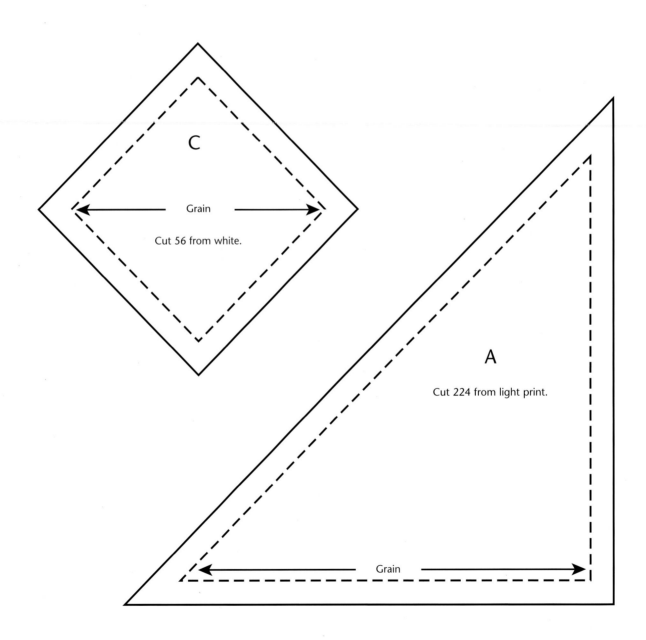

CHAPTER 6

REMEMBERING BELLE EDMONDSON AND OTHER CONFEDERATE SPIES

"I remember once a little old French woman came up from the South (how, nobody knows) who looked the picture of innocence; but she had quilted in her petticoat letters from the boys in gray, the first word many had heard from those loved ones for over two years. She unquilted her petticoat when safe among friends."[68]

Previous page

TODAY'S QUILT PATTERN NAMES were established by women's magazines at the turn of the 20th century. Readers sent designs and recorded local names, but just as often commercial pattern companies made up new names. "Union Star," "Lincoln's Log Home," and "Beauregard Surrounded" are Civil War memories named by the winning side. Few Confederate names exist in the published record, but this collection of new quilts and old represents some of the easiest to decode.

1. *Seven Sisters* by Lucinda Jane Raines Bevill. See page 76.
2. *Richmond Beauty.* See page 74.
3. Dixie Rose block from *Confederate Memorial Quilt* by Terry Clothier Thompson, Lawrence, Kansas, 1998.
4. *Cotton Boll* hand appliquéd and machine quilted by Lori Isenberger, Salida, Colorado, 1999. Lori used antique fabrics and reverse appliqué for her version of an old Carolina pattern. She has inked names of generals from both armies and a Bible verse, "Do not hate your brother in your heart. Do not seek revenge or bear a grudge."
5. *Seven Sisters* by Mary Ellen Nichols, Dickinson, North Dakota, 1988-1998.
6. *Seven Sisters* by Cherie Ralston. See page 78.

Rose O'Neal Greenhow and Belle Boyd are two well-known names from the Civil War's sisterhood of spies. Greenhow, who lived in Union Washington, coiled a message into a courier's hair which revealed Northern battle plans to Confederate General Pierre Beauregard. She is credited with helping win Manassas, the first Southern victory. Yet most tales of spying tell not of military maneuvers, but of smuggled mail and medicine—little acts of bravery like a Missouri girl who told of providing small comforts for a rebel sleeping in the woods whose leg had been broken by a Union bullet.

The old-fashioned quilted petticoats many women wore for warmth provided secret places for gold coins, jewelry, and paper, and fashionable hoop petticoats were even more functional. "Mrs. Houston took dozens of pairs of good warm socks to our loved ones, and we could slip in a little money and medicine wrapped up. She wore hoop skirts, and I tell you they were fine ladders to hang things on."[69]

Women like Mrs. Houston took advantage of the era's chivalry. No man would search a lady. Smuggling and spying required little more of women than looking innocent as they crossed enemy lines. The simplicity of these secret missions is told in stories like that of a Missouri slave who carried notes pinned under her apron, telling Union pickets around the master's house that she was out looking for the cat.

Looking innocent, however, required the bravado to hide a pounding heart and shaking hands. Isabelle Buchanan Edmondson's diaries record the anxious life of a young spy. She lived in Memphis, occupied by Union troops and wrote about dull days in her father's house, where she sewed with her sisters, nieces, and the family's slaves. In the spring of 1864 she had nothing more to do than spend weeks hand-trimming a dress with braid, waiting for opportunities to smuggle "four packages of 300 letters for our Rebel Soldiers." She also carried morphine and chloroform from the city to the Confederate doctors in the country. "Oh Lord deliver me from getting in any trouble with the Yanks."[70]

"Miss Hannah, my young friend, and myself got our horse and we took comforts and pillows. The comforts we folded and laid in the saddles and pulled our riding skirts all over them, so they would not be seen unless we were searched. I took one pillow and Hannah another and tied them under our riding skirts."[71]

Belle, in her mid-twenties during the war, lived on an emotional edge between the excitement of smuggling and days of depressed idleness. She was a thrill seeker, given to wild moods and desperate romanticism. "Misery, despair, destruction," she wrote. She expressed her contempt for the North in her smuggling and in her diary: "May God forgive me if there be sin in hating the Yankees." As the summer of 1864 began, Belle received word she was to be arrested and exiled, so her family arranged her escape to a friend's plantation in Mississippi where she spent the rest of the war.[72]

Mildred Elizabeth Powell (1843-1877) was not as lucky in escaping arrest. Her published diary begins during her confinement for spying. After the Union Army occupied Palmyra, Missouri, she and her neighbors did little to hide their Southern sympathies. "Monday, September 29, 1862. Rose this morning to find our beautiful prairie in front of our dwelling overspread with hostile troops who, like the frogs of Egypt, have covered the land in an hour." Nineteen-year-old Lizzie's spying activities were probably similar to Belle's. She was branded disloyal for encouraging men to fight for the Confederacy and displaying contempt for the army in control of the town. Her contempt continued despite captivity. "To all their questions I gave the most bitter sarcasm for answers that my excited brain could suggest."[73]

Months in jail dampened her spirit and ruined her health. "Gave the guard money to buy me a paper and some reading matter, but he replied . . . he was to let me have no books or papers to assist me in passing away the time. O heaven how can I sleep upon this horrid bed of straw, these offensive, dirty, greasy quilts, these hard pillows of straw. . . . The guards drunken and infuriated made several ineffectual attempts to enter my room and had it not been for a small bolt I had fastened over the lock. . . ."[74]

In solitary confinement with a canary named Robert Lee as her only companion, Lizzie began to cough blood, a symptom of tuberculosis. In February, 1863, her captors relented and banished her to the new state of Nevada, where she could do little to help the Missouri Confederates. She married there and had children, one of whom inherited from her mother "a small Confederate flag, fashioned in prison from bits of ribbon."[75]

A 21-YEAR-OLD MISSOURIAN, identified on the back of the *carte-de-visite* as "Hannah William's mother Grandma Jones," looks the way Lizzie Powell might have when the War began.

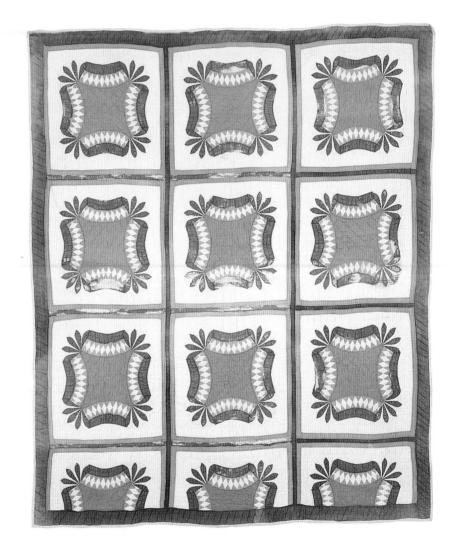

WOMEN LIKE LIZZIE POWELL, who flaunted secessionist sympathies for occupying Union soldiers, might wear a "Secesh Apron."

RICHMOND BEAUTY, maker unknown, 1875-1910, 34" x 34".
Although it's seen better days, the quilt still has much to tell us. It was once green, red, and yellow on white, but the synthetic dyes have faded to a dun-colored peach and khaki. The pattern is all pieced, including the feathers in the corners. In 1942, quilt historian Florence Peto called it "Democrat's Fancy" and noted that the plumes stood for the Democratic Rooster, just like the "Democrat Rose" in Chapter 7. One can almost hear a Rebel yell in the name "Richmond Beauty," published in 1934 by Mrs. Danner's Quilts, a Kansas pattern company. Are the post-Civil War quilts in this design memorials to the Confederate capital and the Lost Cause?

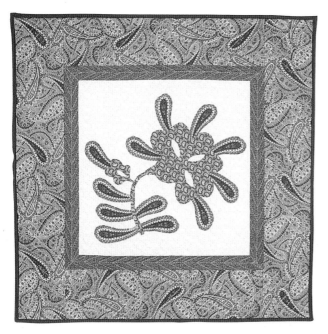

DIXIE ROSE, hand appliquéd and hand quilted by Judy Davis, Lawrence, Kansas, 1999. Judy copied a block from a quilt found during the North Carolina Quilt Project.

THE LADIES OF NEW ORLEANS before GENERAL BUTLER's Proclamation.

After GENERAL BUTLER's Proclamation.

HARPER'S WEEKLY lampooned the ladies of occupied New Orleans in this drawing from the July 12, 1862 issue. Union General Benjamin Butler was so disgusted with Confederate sympathizers' impudence that he threatened to punish those "disreputable women" who exhibited disrespectful behavior with jail time. Few female diarists in the South omitted mention of "Beast" Butler's insult.

HOW TO DEAL WITH FEMALE TRAITORS.

IN DECEMBER, 1861, *Harper's Weekly* suggested punishment for women with secessionist ideas. In one cartoon the artist belittled treason, women, fashion, charity, and Irish servants. Note: "Biddy" (Bridget) relaxing while her mistress does the laundry.

SEVEN SISTERS by Lucinda Jane Raines Bevill (1839-1891), 74" x 96". Puryear, Henry County, Tennessee. Collection of Jeananne Wright. The quilt is thought to have been made during the Civil War, but the fabrics are inconsistent with this story. Particular prints and the solid colors look to be from after 1870, a time when most of the quilts I've seen in this design were made. Did Lucinda consciously make a Southern memorial quilt, or was this just a pretty pattern?

SEVEN SISTERS

Ask a contemporary quiltmaker the pattern name and most respond with "Seven Sisters." Is there a hidden message here—a secret of surviving Dixie spirit? The name may only represent stars in the night sky, an image as old as Greek mythology, which told of the suicidal seven daughters of Atlas who shine forever together in the constellation Taurus. The patchwork pattern itself is older than the Civil War; variations were popular in samplers during the 1840s and 1850s. The earliest published name I've found is "Seven Stars" from the Ladies Art Company's catalog in 1898. "Seven Sisters" was published in the mid-twentieth century, so we may be reading too much 19th-century history into a 20th-century name.

The blue-and-white contemporary version made by Mary Ellen Nichols of Dickinson, North Dakota, has 108 small diamonds in each hexagon block (pictured on page 71). She obtained the pattern she calls "Seven Circle Star" in the best folk tradition. An 88-year-old neighbor gave it to her in 1947 when she was a young bride. Mary Ellen had spent her summers in the Ozarks of South Central Missouri and on a honeymoon trip there she looked up an old friend, Mrs. Stevenson, who gave her the metal template for the diamond. Mary Ellen has never seen the pattern published, and this is her second quilt using the design. It took her ten years to finish the top, as she only pieced it while traveling. The Senior Citizens of Hebron, North Dakota quilted it for her.

"The people of South Central Missouri came into the country from Kentucky and Tennessee sometime before 1850," Mary Ellen wrote me. She was fascinated by their Southern customs and vocabulary. "A bird *used* a tree; candy was put in a *poke*. They didn't use a line to fish with. They stood over the fishing hole and used a three-pronged fork (they called it a *gig*) and got their fish that way. Mrs. Stevenson had her quilting frame hung from the ceiling of her living room. When she was not using it, she pulled it up out of the way."

ACTIVITY FOR RE-ENACTORS: SMUGGLE CONTRABAND SEWING GOODS

Needles, pins, thread, and cloth became almost unobtainable in the South, due to the effective Northern Navy blockade. But ships ran the blockade, and travelers crossing the Mason-Dixon line carried contraband goods from North to South. A Southern lady with an eye to make a little money might be very willing to buy sewing tools and distribute them to her peers for a price.

You probably won't want to smuggle cavalry boots or dress goods (dresses required seven yards of cloth) into camp, but a few yards of silk ribbons and laces, some nice English needles, pins and thimbles, and a little cotton thread would make a profitable inventory for a Southern re-enactor. Store your goods in small calico bags pinned to the bottom of your hoop skirts and steer your conversations to the terrible shortages. Before you know it you'll be tempting the ladies with your contraband. Of course, you'll have to be prepared for the snubs of those who insist they'd never purchase Northern goods, preferring to wear scratchy homespun wool with no trim at all as a sign of their loyalty to the Cause.

"Completely filling the vehicle sat a dignified looking woman. . . . Lifting the edge of her hooped petticoat, she revealed a roll of army cloth, several pairs of cavalry boots, a roll of crimson flannel, packages of gilt braid and sewing silk, cans of preserved meats, a bag of coffee! She was on her way to our own camp, right under the General's nose! . . . It isn't worth while to tell men everything. They are not supposed to be interested in the needle-and-thread ways of women!"

Sara Pryor, a Confederate officer's wife.[76]

"They were fine ladders to hang things on." An illustration from *Frank Leslie's Illustrated Newspaper,* November 22, 1862.

Seven Sisters

Seven Sisters, machine pieced, appliquéd, and quilted by Cherie Ralston, Lawrence, Kansas, 1998.

Lizzie Powell and Belle Edmondson never kept their Confederate sentiments a secret. We can imagine them passing the time spent waiting for smuggling opportunities by stitching a quilt to represent the Confederate flag that was so important to both. Cherie Ralston's quilt was inspired by a secession quilt made by Mrs. Green McPhearson of White County, Arkansas, in the early years of the War. The red and white stripes refer to the "bars" on the first Confederate flag, as well as to the stripes on the Union flag. The stars symbolize the seven states that formed the Confederacy in early 1861. Mrs. McPhearson's quilt had nine stars in the corners, (which included Virginia and Arkansas, the eighth and ninth states to secede). Her quilt is now in the Arkansas Territorial Restoration in Little Rock.[77]

Size: 81" x 78"

FABRIC REQUIREMENTS

BLUE: $1^1/4$ yards for field for stars

RED: $2^1/4$ yards for stripes

WHITE: $2^1/2$ yards for stripes

GOLD: $1^3/4$ yards for stars and binding (or you can cut white stars out of the leftovers from the white stripes)

REMOVABLE MARKER: Test to be sure it is removable on your fabric.

BACKING: $4^3/4$ yards

BATTING: 85" x 82"

CUTTING

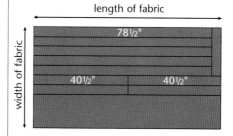

Cutting diagram for red stripes

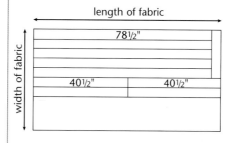

Cutting diagram for white stripes

- Cut 4 strips $5^1/4$" x $40^1/2$" from red.

- Cut 5 strips $5^1/4$" x $78^1/2$" from red.

- Cut 4 strips $5^1/4$" x $40^1/2$" from white.

- Cut 4 strips $5^1/4$" x $78^1/2$" from white.

- Cut 4 squares $19^1/2$" x $19^1/2$" for the blue fields.

- Cut 28 stars using the star template (page 80).

- Cut the backing fabric into two equal lengths. Piece to create backing (page 118).

- Cut 8 strips $2^1/4$" x 42" from gold for binding.

THE QUILT TOP

Stripes

1. Join 2 short red strips (A) and two short white strips (A) alternating red, white, red, white. Make 2.

2. Join 5 long red strips (B) and 4 long white strips (B), alternating red, white, red, and so on.

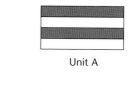

Unit A

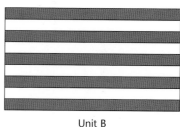

Unit B

Stripe Construction

Stars

1. Mark an 8" circle in the center of the blue square with a removable marker.

2. Appliqué a star in the center and then six stars in a ring around it, using the circle to position the stars as shown in the photograph.

Assembling the Quilt Top

1. Join the blue fields to each end of the A units.

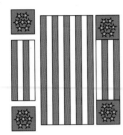

Quilt Construction

2. Join these units to the B unit, referring to the photograph.

QUILTING

1. Layer and baste the quilt (page 119).

2. Cherie machine-quilted a leafy design in the stripes and some freehand swirls behind the stars. She outlined each star $1/4$" inside the seams. Mrs. McPhearson hand-quilted her Secession quilt heavily with stuffed and quilted daisies in the white stripes. She used parallel lines as filler quilting behind the flowers. You might want to quilt five-pointed stars in the stripes or quilt the names of the original Seven Sisters, the first seven states to form the Confederacy: South Carolina, Mississippi, Florida, Alabama, Georgia, Louisiana, and Texas.

3. Bind the quilt (page 119).

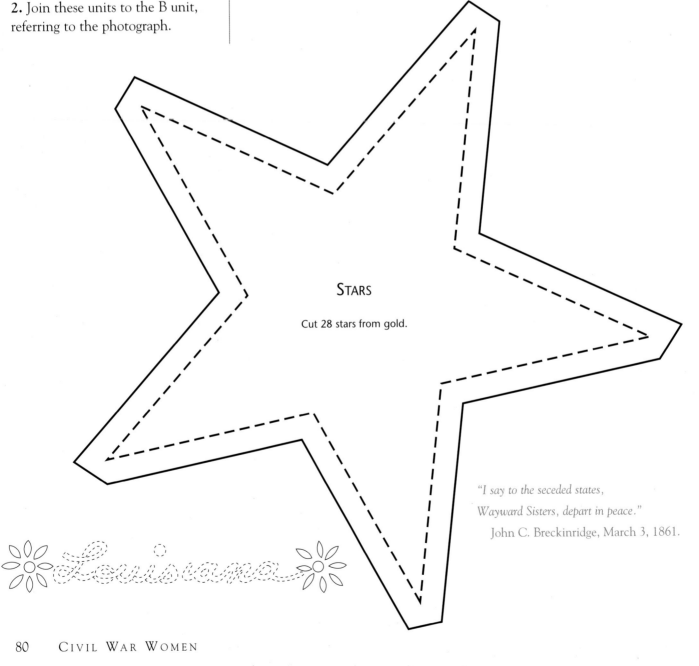

STARS

Cut 28 stars from gold.

"I say to the seceded states,
Wayward Sisters, depart in peace."
John C. Breckinridge, March 3, 1861.

CHAPTER 7

REMEMBERING DOLLY LUNT BURGE AND OTHER PLANTATION OWNERS

"The conscription has robbed almost every household. . . . it was sad to see the homesteads left with only the sad and lonely wife and mother to look after its interests."

Dolly Lunt Burge, Georgia, June 3, 1862.[78]

Dolly Lunt Burge (1817-1891) managed her own plantation long before Fort Sumter. Twice widowed before the war, she spent most of her life as a planter, keeping careful records of her crops in her diary. She also took an interest in politics. The short entry on the day Lincoln defeated Stephen A. Douglas maps the perimeters of her world. She feared the Democrat's loss, "may be the last presidential Election Our United Country will ever see—Digging potatoes."[79]

By the 1860 Presidential election that Dolly Burge feared was the "last election in our United Country," Democrats were in disarray. Stephen Douglas had hoped to win votes in the South with his Kansas-Nebraska bill permitting slavery in new territories, but that political move alienated Northerners so much that Civil War became almost inevitable. The new Republican party nominated Abraham Lincoln to run against Douglas; the Democrats splintered into a third and a fourth party, and Douglas went down in defeat.

Sarah Rousseau Espey of Alabama also worried about disunion as she tracked the rhythms of plantation life before the War. "March 25, 1861. Pretty day . . . our folks [slaves] commenced planting corn; I still feel that strange depression of spirit and dread of coming evil for which I cannot account; it seems that something dreadful is before us. Commenced fringing a counterpane."[80]

Had Dolly and Sarah time to make quilts between planting potatoes and ginning cotton they might have chosen the Democrat Rose, a pattern symbolizing the party of John C. Calhoun, Jefferson Davis, and Stephen A. Douglas. Dolly, born in Maine, adapted easily to Southern culture. She was related to the New England Sumners, of whom Senator Charles Sumner, a Massachusetts Republican, was the most famous member. Southerners hated Sumner for his anti-slavery speeches before the war. After one particularly vehement Senate speech condemning South Carolina, a Democratic Congressman from that state beat him unconscious with a cane on the floor of the Senate.

Previous page
PRE-WAR IMPORTS of French toiles, silks, and chintzes gave way to homespun and sunbonnets in Southern homes. The linen petticoat features the era's trademark cartridge pleats.

A SOUTHERN FAMILY of the planter class in 1863. John Minor Botts of Culpepper County, Virginia, held Union views while living in a Confederate state and was arrested by both sides.

Dolly's Northern birth endowed her with independence, allowing her to act in roles usually held exclusively by Southern men. She moved to Georgia after marrying her first husband. After his death, she married Thomas Burge and actively helped him run his plantation during their eight years together. Burge died in 1858, leaving Dolly with two girls, Lou and Sadai, and the plantation. Although she never was blessed with a long marriage, her three marriages seemed happy (she remarried in 1866). When widowed, she occasionally expressed her loneliness, as in this entry when she was 31 years old. "It has been quite lonely today at home. This keeping house without a man I don't like much. Ah me, how unlike past times, but away with these thoughts."[81]

Dolly was not the type to linger over her losses. Much of her diary as a single woman is filled with short descriptions of her work, the supervision of her slaves on the large farm and cotton cultivation—ginning, picking, selling, and planting cotton. Her wartime political notes express grief over disunion rather than the impractical hopes for Confederate victory often recorded by native Southern diarists. Typical of her estate, however, is Dolly's apology for slavery on the day of Lincoln's re-election in 1864. "If Lincoln is re-elected I think our fate is a hard one. . . . I have never felt that Slavery was altogether right for it is abused by many. . . . The purest and holiest men have owned them & I can see nothing in the Scriptures which forbids it. I have never bought nor sold & have tried to make life easy & pleasant to those that have been bequeathed to me by the dead. I have never ceased to work, but many a Northern housekeeper has a much easier time than a Southern matron with her hundred Negroes."[82]

"Today Jenny came in crying very much, her face bloody and swelled. She said that Fulton [the overseer] had beat her with his fist, because she had not spun a sufficient quantity. It would have distressed you to see her. Oh! How great an evil is slavery."

Maria Bryan, January 27, 1827.[83]

Dolly's daughters were a pleasure to her, although Lou caused concerns, beginning with her adolescent rebellions. "Lou is making a bed quilt but says she is never going to cut up pieces of cloth again for such work that only poor white folks make bed quilts that the rich buy blankets! Martha is spooling some of Webb thread. Such work. I never intend to buy more of Webb's thread!"[84] Concerns over Lou grew serious as she wasted away with tuberculosis. Dolly, Sadai, and the slaves Martha and Mary struggled on after Lou's death, with Dolly keeping accounts of hardship and high prices. "I have hundreds of dollars in my pocket book & yet I cannot buy a yard of calico to make my Sadai a sunbonnet it cannot be had. For weeks she has been wearing a bunch of rags for her bonnet is nothing else. Yesterday however Aunt Polly Davis gave me a peice [sic] of a dress of hers which I shall gladly make up to day."[85]

UNION ARMIES occupying a Southern plantation, 1863.

The Northern embargo on any exports to the South caused shortages of fabric and clothing, and turned everyday items into luxuries. Susan Dabney Smedes, who lived near Vicksburg, Mississippi, remembered wartime substitutions during the last year. "Flour was almost unknown in that part of the Confederacy, coffee and sugar were about as scarce as flour. We had coffee made of peanuts or potatoes, black tea made of blackberry-leaves, and green tea made of holly-leaves. We gave 'war' names to all the varieties of corn-bread that appeared on the table. We had rebel bread, Beauregard cakes, etc. . . . We had scarcely any clothes. A percale apiece at fifteen dollars a yard had been bought as a great bargain; three hundred and fifty dollars had been given for a purple calico dress for Sophy."[86]

The many published Southern diaries follow a typical pattern, with women left alone to complain of poor crops, poor help, inflation, hunger, and homespun. Bad turns to worse and worse turns to disaster as the Yankees overrun the country. "Like demons they rush in. My yards are full. To my smoke house, my Dairy, Pantry, kitchen and cellar like famished wolves they come, breaking locks and whatever is in their way."[87]

One of the Civil War stories passed to our generation is the tale about burying the quilts with the silver to hide the heirlooms from the Yankees. Diaries, letters, and memoirs record the scurrying around as rumors of Union soldiers reached the plantations. Susan Smedes "set to work to bury the money and silver. Large hoops were in fashion at this time, and we tied our silver in bags and put these under our hoops and went out one May day a mile from the house to a rock-quarry. Here we dug a hole with the dinner-knives that we had secreted about our persons for the purpose, and in this hole we placed our valuables. Then we put over them the largest stone that six or seven girls could move."[88]

The white property owners trusted their African-American workers to keep treasures safe from Yankee pillagers. "Sadai was giving our clothes to the servants to hide in their cabins. Silk dresses challis muslins & merinos linens and hoseiry [sic] all found their way into the chests of the women & under their beds. China Silver was all laid away under ground & Sadai bid Mary to hid [sic] a bit of soap under some bricks."[89] "Some of our friends had buried their watches, and so destroyed them. We sewed up our watches and such valuables as would be spoiled by dampness in the form of a bustle, and gave it to our trusted Aunt Abby [a slave] to wear."[90]

THE CAPTION says "Searching for Arms in a Rebel's House," but few soldiers resisted the urge to plunder.

The Union Army viewed the occupation from a different perspective. Thomas W. Higginson, who commanded a Union regiment of former slaves, recorded their exploits as they marched through coastal Beaufort, Georgia, to Fernandina, Florida. One morning Higginson and a corporal came upon a plantation run by a widow from Philadelphia. Higginson took great delight in presenting "Corporal Robert Sutton" to his former mistress. "I never saw a finer bit of unutterable indignation than came over the face of my hostess, as she slowly recognized him. She drew herself up, and dropped out the monosyllables of her answer as if they were so many drops of nitric acid. 'Ah,' quoth my lady, 'we called him Bob!'"[91]

ACTIVITY FOR RE-ENACTORS: STAGE A BAZAAR

WOMEN SELLING NICK-NACKS at the tables of the New York Metropolitan Fair in 1864.

Bazaars were the bastion of female fundraising in both North and South. Once the war began, women converted traditional ladies' fairs, which had raised money for church building projects and reform causes, to war relief efforts. In the South women conducted Gunboat Fairs, a short-lived effort to support the Confederate Navy. By the end of war, Union Christmas bazaars had evolved into enormous events called Sanitary Fairs that raised money for the Sanitary Commission's work with sick and wounded soldiers. Re-enactors might want to stage a Sanitary Fair, but an army of civilians would be required to produce an extravaganza like New York's 1864 Metropolitan Fair, which lasted weeks, covered blocks of cityscape, and raised hundreds of thousands of dollars.

A more manageable activity might be a smaller bazaar such as the "Last Fair," held in Columbia, South Carolina, in January, 1865. Amarintha and Isabella Snowden, leaders of the Soldiers' Relief Association of Charleston, began preparing for the fundraiser in the fall of 1864. Grace Brown Elmore, like several other Confederate diarists, helped stage this last denial of defeat, which was held "notwithstanding the rains, the floods, the sweeping away of hail wads and the steady approach of the Yankee. . . . The house, Mother says, is bazaar mad. . . . so many letters to be written, so many tobacco pouches to be made." Her descriptions give us an idea of how a reproduction fair might be decorated: "On each side of the hall . . . booths draped in the gayest colors red and white or blue, garlanded with evergreens, and filled with all sorts of nick nacks." Each Confederate state was represented by a tent, although the crafts sold there were locally made. "Everybody left bad spirits and anxiety at the door, if Sherman was mentioned 'twas in a most casual way, nobody had time for blues."[92]

Emma LeConte also noted the fair in her diary. "Our great bazaar opened last night, and such a jam! . . . The tables or booths are tastefully draped with damask and lace curtains, and elaborately decorated with evergreens. To go in there one would scarce believe it was war times. The tables are loaded with fancy articles—brought through the blockade, or manufactured by the ladies. . . cakes, jellies, creams, candies . . . They had intended holding it for two weeks, but Sherman's proximity forces them to hurry up. I heard . . . that the aforesaid individual had announced his intention of attending the Ladies' Bazaar in person before it closes."[93]

To conduct a fair you must secure a hall and decorate it. Red, white, and blue bunting and evergreens seem to have been the standards. Garlands were an important part of the era's fashion, not only at Christmas, but also at other festivities and even for everyday parlor decor. Photographs and drawings of interiors show more than the coniferous pine boughs we hang at Christmas. Victorians considered live ivy and trailing philodendrons appropriate drapery for everything from hospital wards to ballrooms.

The fair's major function is to "exchange nick-nacks for greenbacks." You must have donated items to sell and volunteers to sell them at tables. Handmade tobacco pouches, pincushions, housewifes (sewing kits), quilts, and homemade toys were good sellers. Parthenia Vardaman recalled her days of crocheting capes, sacques, vandykes, shawls, gloves, socks, stockings, and men's suspenders for the fairs.[94]

"Each table had something costly, one a handsome crape shawl given by Mrs. Gen. Joe Johnston, another a silver ladle, another a beautiful brooch, plenty of showy worsted work [possibly Berlin work or needlepoint pictures], some paintings, good deal of clothing, doll babies and toys just from Europe. . . . knives, scissors, needles & thread that had run the blockade. Any quantity of cloth dolls, home manafacture [sic] and home toys of all sorts."

Grace Brown Elmore.[95]

HARPER'S WEEKLY covered the Metropolitan Fair so well we can imagine how to decorate.

Democrat Rose

Democrat Rose, hand appliquéd and hand
quilted by Nancy P. Wakefield,
Platte City, Missouri, 1999.

This floral appliqué, a cockscomb and rose variation, was a popular design from about 1840 to 1880. We've added a border of roosters. The tail of the cock is the same shape as the cockscomb around the central flower. Quilt historian Florence Peto speculated that combs in patterns named for Democrats stood for the rooster which once symbolized the party. Before Thomas Nast drew a Democratic donkey in 1870, Democrats knew to vote for the candidate with a rooster by his name. The common understanding of the rooster's role is evident in a satirical view of the new jail written by the editor of the Quindaro, Kansas, *Tribune*, a Republican newspaper. "On the top there will be placed a beautiful statue of the Goddess of Liberty, who will hold in one hand a 'Democratic Rooster' to tell which way the wind blows."[96]

Make the Democrat Rose to remember the women of the South and, as you sew, imagine a scenario if women had been able to vote in 1860.

Size: 46" x 46"

Center medallion, 30" x 30"

Border, 8"

FABRIC REQUIREMENTS

LIGHT-COLORED PRINT: 1 yard for the center medallion

RED-AND-BLACK PLAID: 10" x 10" scrap for center medallion flower

RED-AND-BLACK PRINT: 8" x 8" scrap for center medallion flower

YELLOW PRINT #1: 5" x 5" for center circle in medallion center

YELLOW PRINT #2: ¹/₂ yard for roosters' tails in the border and cockscombs in the center medallion

BLACK PRINT #1: 5" x 5" for center medallion center

BLACK PRINT #2: ³/₄ yard for roosters' bodies and binding

GREEN PRINT: ¹/₂ yard for stems

BLACK, RED, YELLOW, AND GREEN SCRAPS: for leaves, buds, and flowers

LIGHT-COLORED PRINT: 1¹/₃ yards for the border

BACKING: 3 yards

BATTING: 50" x 50"

CUTTING

- Cut one square 34" x 34" from the light-colored print for the center medallion. Trim to 30¹/₂" x 30¹/₂" after the appliqué is complete.

- Cut one using template A on page 91 from red-and-black plaid.

- Cut one using template B on page 91 from red-and-black print.

- Cut one using template C on page 91 from black print #1.

- Cut one using template D on page 91 from yellow print #1.

- Cut 10 using template E on page 92 from yellow print #2.

- Cut 8 using template F on page 90 from red scraps.

- Cut 8 using template G on page 90 from yellow scraps.

- Cut 10 using template H on page 92 from black print #2.

- Cut 12 using templates I and J on page 91 from red scraps.

- Cut 40 using template K on page 91 from green scraps.

- Cut approximately 12 feet of 1¹/₄" bias strips from green print for the stems.

- Cut 2 lengthwise strips 8¹/₂" x 30¹/₂" from the light-colored print for the top and bottom borders.

- Cut 2 lengthwise strips 8¹/₂" x 46¹/₂" from the light-colored print for the side borders.

- Cut the backing fabric into two equal lengths. Piece to create backing (page 118).

- Cut 5 strips 2¹/₄" x 42" from black print #2 for the binding.

THE QUILT TOP

Center Medallion

1. Press the background fabric in half vertically and horizontally. Then open it and press it in half diagonally (from corner to corner) in both directions. This will help you position the appliqué pieces.

2. Position the center flower unit and the four corner flowers before you place the stems and combs, referring to the photograph. Finish by placing the leaves and buds.

3. Appliqué the pieces to the background (page 116).

4. Trim to $30\frac{1}{2}$" x $30\frac{1}{2}$".

Border

1. Sew the shorter border strips to the top and bottom of the block. Then add longer side strips.

2. Using the photograph for reference, space the ten roosters as shown and appliqué. Appliqué the border flower stems over the seams.

QUILTING

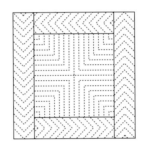

Quilting Design

1. Layer and baste the quilt (page 119).

2. Nancy quilted her piece in old-fashioned elbow quilting (right angle quilting) behind the appliqué. See the appliqué patterns for the designs she used on top of the flowers and roosters. She quilted a chevron design, another version of elbow quilting in the border.

3. Bind the quilt (page 119).

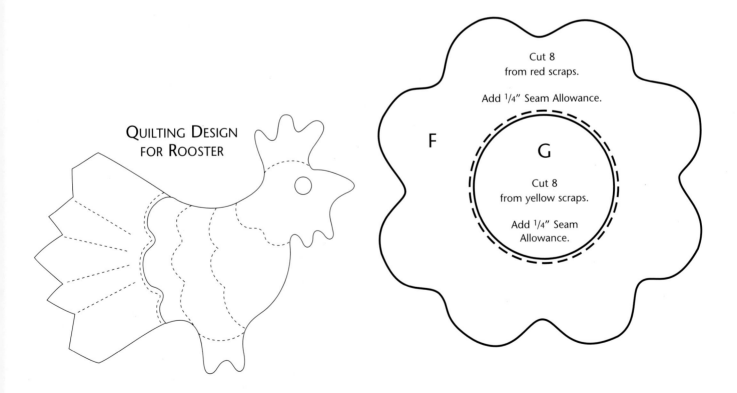

QUILTING DESIGN FOR ROOSTER

F

G

Cut 8 from red scraps.

Add $\frac{1}{4}$" Seam Allowance.

Cut 8 from yellow scraps.

Add $\frac{1}{4}$" Seam Allowance.

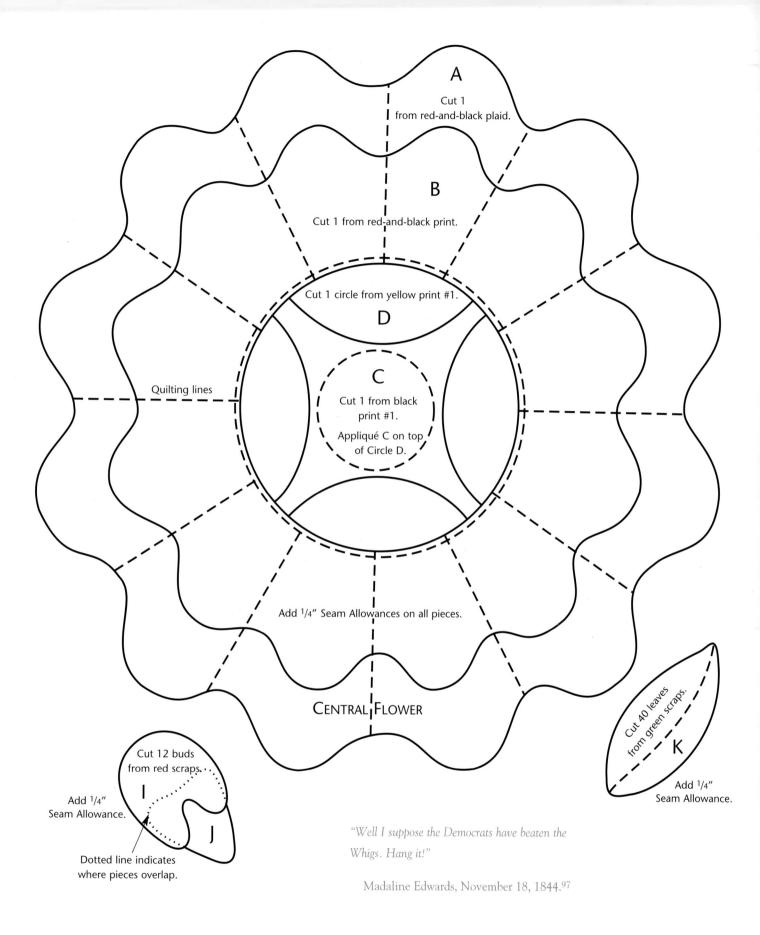

A

Cut 1
from red-and-black plaid.

B

Cut 1 from red-and-black print.

Cut 1 circle from yellow print #1.

D

C

Cut 1 from black
print #1.

Appliqué C on top
of Circle D.

Quilting lines

Add ¹/4″ Seam Allowances on all pieces.

CENTRAL FLOWER

Cut 40 leaves
from green scraps.

K

Add ¹/4″
Seam Allowance.

Cut 12 buds
from red scraps.

I

J

Add ¹/4″
Seam Allowance.

Dotted line indicates
where pieces overlap.

*"Well I suppose the Democrats have beaten the
Whigs. Hang it!"*

Madaline Edwards, November 18, 1844.[97]

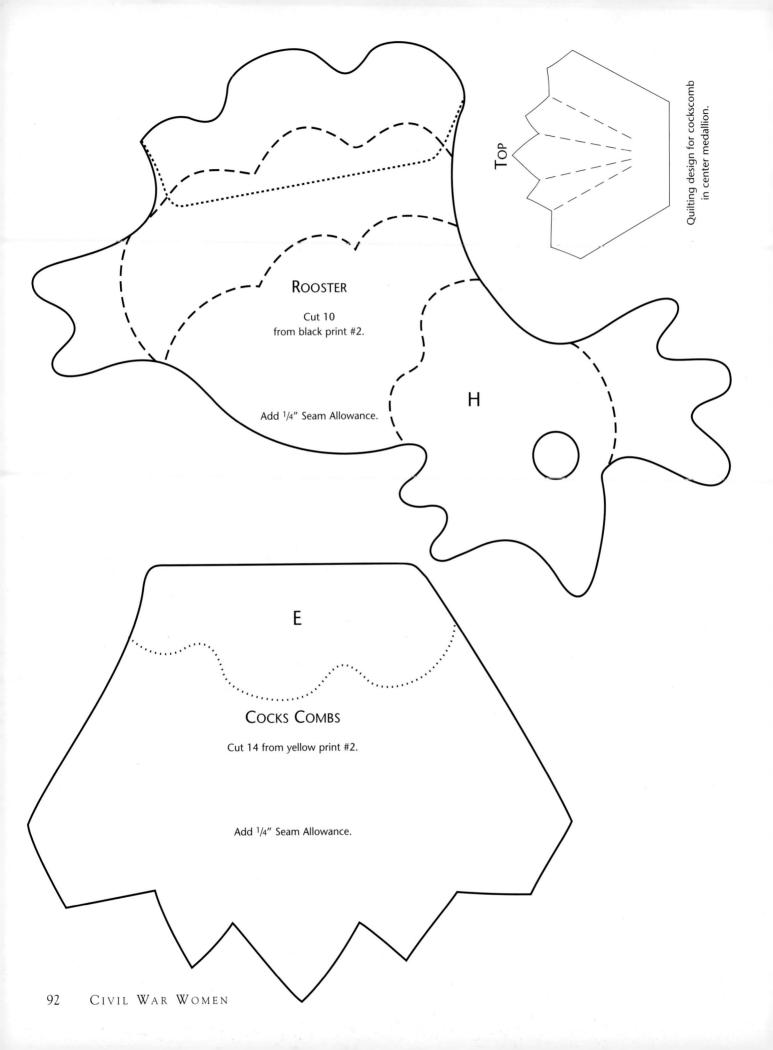

Quilting design for cockscomb in center medallion.

Top

ROOSTER

Cut 10
from black print #2.

Add 1/4" Seam Allowance.

H

E

COCKS COMBS

Cut 14 from yellow print #2.

Add 1/4" Seam Allowance.

CHAPTER 8

REMEMBERING BABE SIMS AND OTHER GOVERNMENT CLERKS

"I have been in the treasury department now for nearly a month. . . . You will readily perceive that my penmanship has been detrimentally affected by my stay among the bank notes, but alas too true. We have to write so fast that I am getting into signing my name 3200 times everyday."
  Leora Sims, June 22, 1864.[98]

The traditional image of Civil-War-era girls and women is largely symbolic. Like Jeff Davis's daughter Maggie in the little quilt, girls were viewed as images of loyalty and liberty holding an American flag. The pictures do not capture young women's real lives. Girls like Babe Sims lived through radical changes in status, from pampered daughters of privilege to independent survivors who were responsible for their own living and often that of the family.

As the War approached, 18-year-old Leora Amanda Sims was a fortunate child of the South. Nicknamed "Babe" by friends and family, she came from a family of girls indulged by their father, a South Carolina landowner. She was a graduate of the South's exclusive finishing school, Barhamville in Columbia. There she formed lifelong friendships with other girls of her class, among them Harriet Palmer, who preserved Babe's letters describing South Carolina's capitol city from just before Secession to the years of Reconstruction.[99]

We glimpse Babe's beauty in her own letters and those of Harriett's. Blonde and petite, her size was probably the inspiration for her nickname. No one ever seemed to call her Leora. In pre-war days, Babe's life was "one continual round of enjoyment." She asked the more practical Harriet, "Do you not think I am very silly and talk too much about men?" She had her pick of the boys in Columbia, but she had a knack for bad choices. There was Wallace, who drank, and Willie, whose offenses weren't mentioned: "I could tell you something bout W.G. that would make you almost cry for your old friend, but never mind."

At first, Babe viewed war as a social event. While the South Carolina legislature debated secession after Lincoln's election in late 1860, she listened in the balconies. She told Harriett she'd named a new black horse "Secession." "I wonder if your Southern blood is as fiery as mine. I am a regular fire-eater." Babe's enthusiasm waned during the first year of the War. "Politics," she wrote, "engrosses my almost every thought. Our beloved Carolina is now an asylum for imps that even Hell cannot surpass. . . . I hope this is not profanity!"

Previous page
JEFF DAVIS'S DAUGHTER, machine appliqued and machine quilted by Barbara Eikmeier, Leavenworth, Kansas, 1999. Barbara's miniature portrait of Maggie Davis is photographed with typical children's clothing. The small turkey red wrapper is bordered with a serpentine stripe. Like the purple print dress, the figure is a foulard, a French-style scarf print. The double-pink print in the dress on the lower left was a staple of girls' wardrobes and their mothers' quilts.

After a long gap in letters to Harriet she described a serious depression in the winter of 1862-3. "My darling friend, I have passed through hours, even days and weeks, when my mind has been so clouded, even reason itself seemed to totter. I have always been one to look on the sunny side but doubts arose as to my very own existence." She seemed to realize that she was affected by what psychologists today label manic-depression or bipolar disorder. "I believe those who are of an enthusiastic nature when overwhelmed suffer more deeply than those of a more passive temperament." Over the next few years, her moods alternated with complaints typical of the upper class, rather than of the truly poor. She decried shortages of clothing and eligible men rather than starvation and family deaths. "We are arranging our wardrobe for the summer turning things inside out, making new things out of old. A cousin of mine. . . says the ladies of the South need not fear, for according to statistics there are a surplus of 720 thousand men more than ladies in the South. For my own part I will be an old maid."

AN UNKNOWN YOUNG WOMAN photographed in Manchester, Iowa.

While her father fought in Arkansas, Babe spent the first war years teaching the children of the family, confined to the house with her lonely mother. Her vistas broadened when the War grew closer to Columbia. In 1864, she nursed injured soldiers who arrived daily on the trains, a sad task that gave her life more meaning. "Poor fellows, they are so patient and many of them are so mangled. We have some romantic times with them too."

In that same letter she tells Harriet that she has a second job as a clerk in the Confederate Treasury. The Secretary, Christopher Memminger, hired women to replace the male clerks conscripted away from their desks to fight in the Treasury Department Battalion. John Beauchamp Jones, secretary to the Confederate Secretary of War in Richmond, Virginia, noted the feminization of his department in his diary. "Many ladies have been appointed clerks. There is a roomful of them just over the Secretary's office, and he says they distract him with their noise of moving of chairs and running about, etc."[100]

UNION AND CONFEDERATE GIRLS were encouraged to withhold their affections from "slackers."

Female clerks were not strictly a wartime innovation. In 1855, the U.S. Patent Office hired women to copy documents by hand. Clara Barton, later a noted Civil War nurse, and Ellen Lloyd Blunt, widowed daughter of Francis Scott Key, worked there until the Secretary of the Interior re-evaluated the situation. Objecting to mixing the sexes in the workplace, he decreed women retreat to their homes where they would be paid at piecework rates of ten cents per hundred words.

During the War the Post Offices, War Departments, and other bureaus North and South hired women, but it was Memminger's Treasury Girls who received the most attention. With her aristocratic background and family contacts, Babe Sims was a typical Treasury Girl, "one of the high-born ladies of the land." Clerkships, despite their hand-numbing duties, were political plums awarded to sustain society's women who had fallen on hard times. Applications were numerous, interviews excruciating, and examinations exacting. But the most important qualification was political connection. John Beauchamp Jones noted that when women clerkships became available in his War Department, even President Davis made a recommendation "who, of course, will be appointed." [101]

"A visit to Mr. Memminger, whose stolid and apparently unsympathizing face ever produced an unpleasant impression on the beholder, was sometimes undertaken by a woman more courageous than her sisters, to be attended with nervous apprehension when in his sight, and often by weeping when the ordeal was over."

Sallie Brock Putnam, 1867.[102]

For most of the War, the Treasury operated in the Confederate Capitol at Richmond. Fearing Yankee confiscation of banknote shipments when fighting moved deeper into the South, Secretary Memminger moved the women's department to Columbia, closer to the printing offices. Treasury Girls protested with pleas and petitions, but Memminger gave them a choice of evacuating to South Carolina or losing their jobs. Among the new workers hired in Columbia was Babe Sims.

Treasury Girls handled bank notes and bonds. During the first three years of the Confederacy, each note and bond was signed by hand, some twice. We might assume that the women signed Treasurer John N. Hendren's name to the notes, but Babe told Harriett she was signing her own name 3200 times a day. Clerks also numbered, clipped, packed, and shipped the paper documents and kept registers of the notes and bonds and of their cancellations. By War's end, over eighty million notes and eight hundred thousand bonds had passed through Memminger's offices.

We consider chronic hand pain a consequence of the computer age, but clerks like Babe in the Confederacy and Caroline Colton in Columbus, Ohio, described familiar complaints. After hours of listing mustering out rolls, Lina Colton wrote her sister, "I have handled the pen so much, of late, that today—well I do not know what is the matter but my fingers seem <u>kind of stiff</u> and it is rather difficult to <u>write</u> just now."[103]

Repetitive motion syndrome was not the only familiar complaint. After the War, Alice Caton, a clerk in the Federal Treasury, swore an affidavit against the United States Senator from Kansas, stating that "having procured me employment [he] did approach me with dishonorable offers and for fear I might lose my place I did go with said Hon. S. C. Pomeroy to Baltimore, Maryland and slept in bed with him in Room 155 in Barnum's Hotel, and that said Pomeroy did have criminal connections with me during the night of February 29, 1868."[104]

Babe's job disappeared with the destruction of Columbia in February, 1865. When Sherman's Union troops swept through the city, they spared the Sims's house, but the devastation forced the family to shelter in Spartanburg, where they discussed moving to Mexico or Brazil. Babe's sister took over her correspondence because Babe was again too depressed to write. "Her health is very feeble and the great change in our circumstances and the downfall of the Confederacy seemed to weigh on her spirits that she was not herself for sometime, so gloomy and melancholy. Her private sorrows too seemed too deep for her at this time."

Like many other Southerners, Babe looked west after the War, spending time in Council Bluffs, Iowa, with family friends. Two years after Columbia's fall, she was back in the city, on "the shady side of 25" but able to see the sun. "I am so happy now, and if we are very poor and the struggle for mere necessities is not over I would not change my place with the Rothschilds. . . . Have you given up the idea of matrimony? I have and will have to go to make a living for myself. My father is shattered mentally and physically and although he has a great deal of land it is not now doing anyone a particle of good."

Her short experience as a Treasury Girl widened her horizons beyond that of a traditional Southern belle and wife. Much to her surprise, she found employment as a clerk in a store near the State House. The Sims sisters tried restoring the old Barhamville School for classes for veterans' daughters. There Babe's letters stop. She fades from the Palmer's papers in 1870 as she takes a job as a governess, and we hear almost incidentally that she married Richard O'Neale Jr. in the early 1870s.

ACTIVITY FOR RE-ENACTORS:
MAKE A SWEETHEART FLAG

"April, 18th, 1864. Well I expect our days of peace and quiet are over, another squad of Yanks passed. . . . I promised to make a Confederate Flag for one of them, Mr. Greer, and he promised he would not reenlist. So I have spent the evening making one, and will give it next time he comes."

Belle Edmondson. [105]

Each town company and militia was proud of the flags stitched by local women. Many women's Civil War diaries begin with an account of the ceremony presenting a handmade flag to the regiment. A woman might present a pocket-sized flag, called a sweetheart flag, to a son or husband as he returned to the battlefield. She might mail him one in a letter to carry with his pocket Bible and her daguerreotype portrait. How many widows found the small flag among the dead man's possessions shipped back from the field hospital?

A woman in camp could spend her time hand-stitching a small flag, Confederate or Union. The flags go together quickly. You might want to embroider or ink the stars rather than appliqué them. Remember that the standardized Union flag we know with its 13 red and white stripes and a blue field of stars representing each state is a twentieth-century convention. Nineteenth-century flags allowed wonderful latitude. Use the patterns given for Maggie Davis's flags (see flags on the quilt pattern on page 101 and 103). You may prefer to vary the stars and stripes the way Civil War-era seamstresses often did. To finish the flags, bind the edges or make two flags and stitch them back to back so the sweetheart flag is reversible.

Ideas for Flags:

1. Appliqué one white star in a blue field.

2. Make the stripes of striped fabric and don't worry about the number. Red and white is good, but consider blue and white or blue and red. You can push the symbol in all directions and it still reads as an American flag

3. Make the stripes of wavy striped fabric, making it look like it's blowing in the wind.

4. Make the field of a blue-and-white print. One common indigo print in those days featured a tiny six-pointed white star. Today we can buy lots of fabrics with five-pointed stars printed on them.

5. Appliqué or ink a word—"Union," "Secession," "Liberty," or "State's Rights" depending on your sweetheart's convictions—across the stripes or the field.

6. Ink the regiment's name along a white stripe or put one star in the field and ink the name in the center.

7. Make the field white and ink a symbol on it—an eagle for a Union man, a palmetto for a South Carolinian.

PEACE AND UNITY with Karina by Shauna Christensen, Lawrence, Kansas, 1999. Shauna photo-transferred a portrait of her daughter Karina to fabric and turned Maggie Davis's image into Karina in Civil War costume. While stitching images from the patterns in Chapters 7 and 8 and a pieced border in the Underground Railroad design, she imagined a time when teenagers might have been easier to raise.

Jeff Davis's Daughter

Jeff Davis's Daughter, hand appliquéd and
hand quilted by Nancy Hornback,
Wichita, Kansas, 1998.

Maggie was the darling of the Davis family and the Confederacy. Her father wrote of her in a letter to former President Franklin Pierce, "*My dear friend. Our children have grown rapidly and the little girl is now quite a companion to me when at evening I go home to forget the past and postpone the future.*" January 17, 1859.

Margaret Davis was Jefferson and Varina Davis's oldest child, born in Washington in 1855, when her father was Secretary of War under Pierce. Maggie's portrait is drawn from a block in a sampler quilt dated November 18th, 1867, six months after the former President of the Confederacy was released from Federal Prison. The original quilt, made in New York, depicts Davis being greeted by his daughter with the words "Jeff Davis and Daughter" embroidered between them. Maggie holds an American flag, symbolizing the return of the South to the Union. A second sampler quilt, more primitive than the first, also contains a block of Maggie Davis holding a flag. The trees, birds, and butterflies here are drawn from the New York quilt. Maggie's mother made a quilt about that time with a butterfly in the center—the symbol, her granddaughter wrote, for "the soul of the Confederacy, beautiful and immortal."[106]

Size: 57" x 57"

Nine blocks, various sizes

Sashing strips, 1 1/2" finished

Border, 4 1/2" finished

FABRIC REQUIREMENTS

LIGHT-COLORED FABRIC: 17" x 17" squares of nine different fabrics for the block backgrounds

PRINT FABRICS: 10" x 10" squares of seven different fabrics for the dresses

GREEN PRINT: 2 fat quarters for the grass and trees

RED-AND-WHITE STRIPED FABRIC: 1/4 yard of red-and-white striped fabric **or** strip piece your own of red and white fabric as Nancy did for the flags

SCRAPS: for hair, faces, hands, collars, flag poles, socks, shoes or boots, butterflies, birds, and cherries.

DARK BLUE SOLID: 1 1/2 yards for sashing and binding

PRINT FABRIC: 1 3/4 for the border. (There will be some left over.) Nancy used a foulard.

BACKING: 3 1/2 yards

BATTING: 61" x 61"

CUTTING

Note: We've included a Confederate flag (page 101) in case you want to make an unreconstructed version of the First Daughter of the Confederacy.

- Trace and cut the appliqué pieces, adding 1/4" seam allowances (pages 101-104). You'll need seven Maggies with flags, one cherry tree, twenty-four cherries, one oak tree, two butterflies, and two birds.

- Trim the Maggie blocks to 14 1/2" x 14 1/2" and the tree blocks to 16" x 14 1/2".

- Cut 4 lengthwise strips 2" x 14 1/2" from dark blue solid for the short vertical sashing.

- Cut 6 lengthwise strips 2" x 47" from dark blue solid for the long vertical and horizontal sashing.

- Cut 4 lengthwise strips 5" x 60" from the print border fabric.

- Cut the backing fabric into two equal lengths. Piece to create backing (page 118).

- Cut 6 strips 2 1/4" x 42" from the dark blue solid for the binding.

THE QUILT TOP

Appliqué

1. Press the background fabric in half vertically and horizontally. Then open it and press it in half diagonally (from corner to corner) in both directions. Position the appliqué pieces, referring to the photograph. Appliqué the figures and trees onto the block backgrounds (page 116). Trim the blocks to size. Appliqué the butterflies and birds after the three center blocks are sewn together.

Sashing

1. Referring to the quilt photograph, lay out the blocks and sashing strips.

2. Join a tree block to each side of a Maggie block. Press. Appliqué the butterflies and birds.

3. Attach the short vertical sashing between the remaining Maggie blocks, making two rows of three blocks. Press.

4. Join the rows with horizontal sashing between the rows. Press.

Borders

1. Stitch the dark blue sashing border strips to the border strips. Attach to the quilt top and miter the corners (page 118). Press.

QUILTING

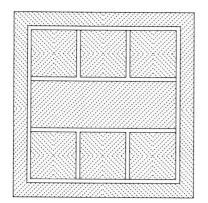

Quilting Design

1. Layer and baste the quilt (page 119).

2. Nancy quilted an outline around each appliqué shape, including the flags. In each block she quilted lines of elbow quilting, as shown, but she did not quilt across the figures. In the center rectangle and the borders she quilted diagonal lines. You may want to double your quilting lines as they did in the mid-nineteenth century.

3. Bind the quilt (page 119).

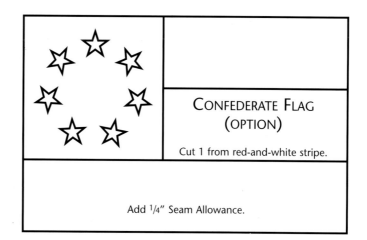

CONFEDERATE FLAG (OPTION)

Cut 1 from red-and-white stripe.

Add ¼″ Seam Allowance.

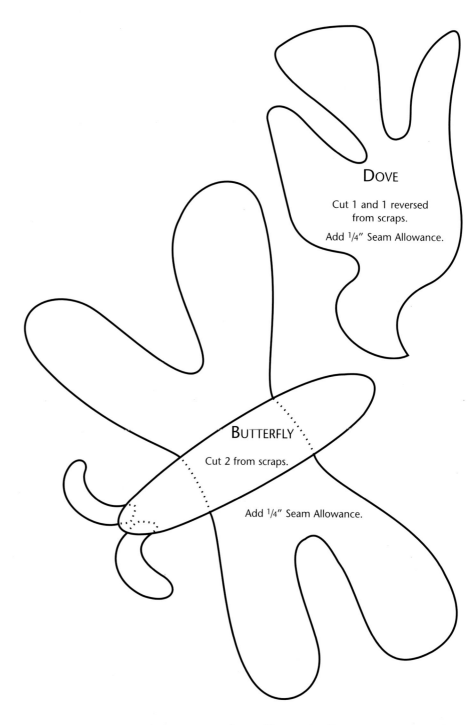

DOVE

Cut 1 and 1 reversed from scraps.

Add ¼″ Seam Allowance.

BUTTERFLY

Cut 2 from scraps.

Add ¼″ Seam Allowance.

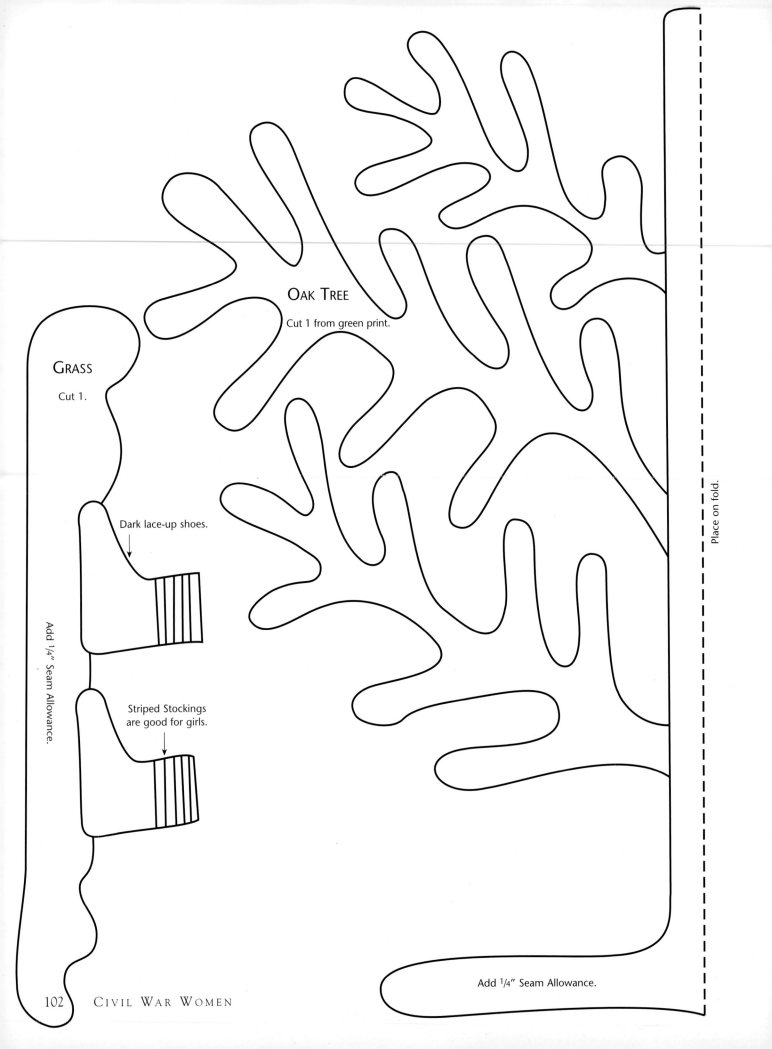

OAK TREE

Cut 1 from green print.

GRASS

Cut 1.

Dark lace-up shoes.

Striped Stockings
are good for girls.

Add ¼" Seam Allowance.

Place on fold.

Add ¼" Seam Allowance.

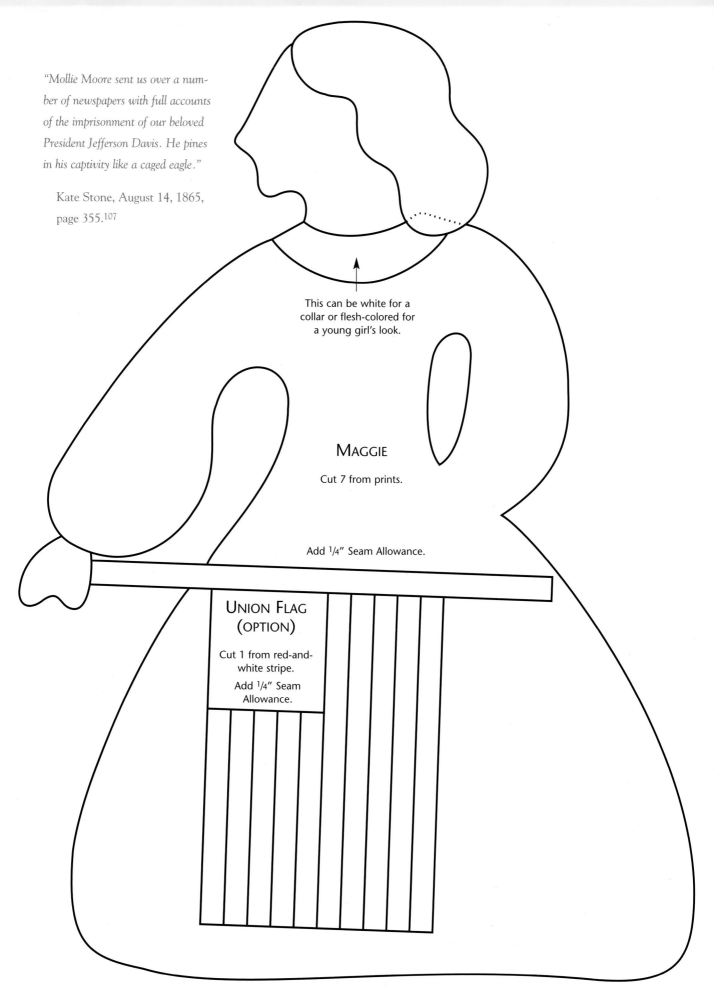

This can be white for a collar or flesh-colored for a young girl's look.

MAGGIE

Cut 7 from prints.

Add ¼" Seam Allowance.

UNION FLAG (OPTION)

Cut 1 from red-and-white stripe.

Add ¼" Seam Allowance.

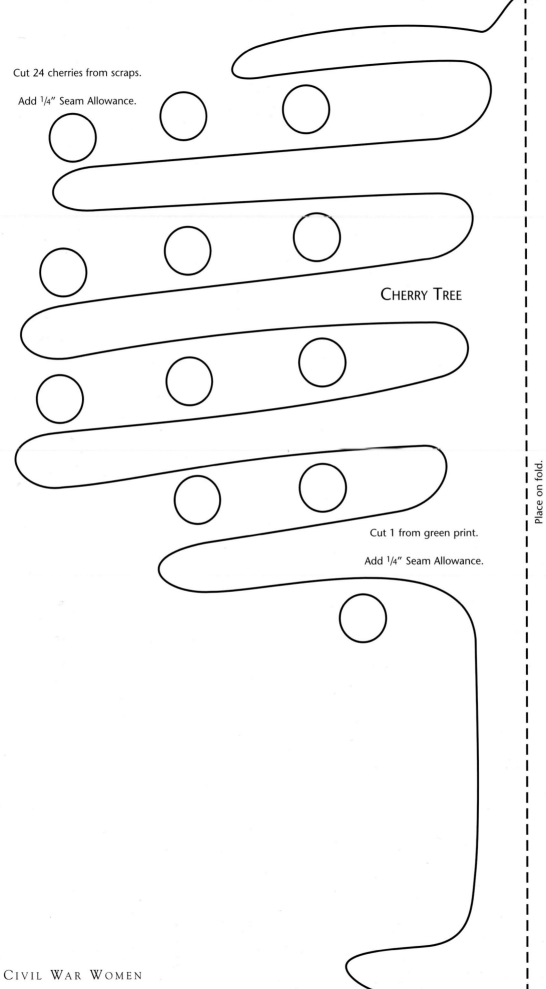

Cut 24 cherries from scraps.

Add 1/4" Seam Allowance.

CHERRY TREE

Cut 1 from green print.

Add 1/4" Seam Allowance.

Place on fold.

CHAPTER 9

REMEMBERING RACHEL CORMANY AND OTHER SOLDIERS' WIVES

*"Mar 13, 1863. Quite cold—put a cradle quilt in the frame—Rec'd another letter from Samuel…
Feel pretty happy. Samuel writes such good letters. March 14. Pleasant. Not so cold. I baked and
ironed and finished the quilting on the cradle quilt. Rec'd papers from My Saml. O! such
good ones."*

Rachel Cormany.[108]

For wives waiting at home, needlework was many things—a profession, war
work, and a private refuge from their stressful lives. Rachel Bowman Cormany
recorded a good deal about her needlework but, like too many diarists, shared
no information about the patterns or colors of her quilts. Was the cradle quilt
for baby Cora or a commission from a customer? Because Rachel lived in Ohio
and Pennsylvania we can assume her quilt was the appliqué typical of the
region. We can also imagine that a woman with Rachel's political sensibilities,
one who'd attended Oberlin College and worked in the Underground Railroad
before the war, would have chosen a pattern symbolizing the Union.

We can also imagine quite clearly Rachel's war-time role, as a soldier's wife,
thanks to the era's art and literature. The waiting wife was the subject of good
art and bad, high art and low, from Louisa May Alcott's *Little Women* and
Thomas Nast's drawings for *Harper's Weekly* to the sentimental poetry in all
the newspapers. We can empathize with the army wife's pain and loneliness,
her terror of losing her husband, joys at furloughs, and final peace. We also
have Rachel's diary, a litany of emotional ups and downs. "Since I last wrote
in my journal I have been very busy sewing and getting ready to go visit my
dear precious husband in the army on the Potomac. Last Monday was the day
set to start, but to my great joy he came to visit me—Arrived here on last
Monday noon. . . . As soon as dinner was over we had to say 'Goodbye.' How
could I prevent those tears even if the room was full of people. . . . All after-
noon in spite of me the tears would come."

Previous page
RACHEL CORMANY passed her time
sewing and fashioning wreaths of hair.
Feather wreaths were also popular crafts
during the war. The baby's dress sports
"calico" buttons, as the spotted buttons
were then known.

Financial desperation added to the emotional whirlwinds. Women who began the War as part of the growing middle class fell into deep poverty by Appomatox. Rachel survived on her husband's pay of $8 per month by boarding with relatives and sewing for cash. In 1863, the spring she made the cradle quilt, she and Cora lived in Chambersburg, Pennsylvania, 25 miles east of Gettysburg. In June, Rachel suddenly found herself at War's center. Confederate General Robert E. Lee took an offensive march into Northern territory, his armies occupying Chambersburg. Soldiers used the town as a staging area for the battle at Gettysburg. Rachel recorded the details of those "eventful days," when cannonading punctuated the daily housework of a woman with a young child. On July 3rd, while the decisive battle raged nearby, she wrote, "Went to Mammy Royers & got some peas & new potatoes. . . . There are no rebels in town today except the sick."

Rachel lived on letters and rumors. After a hurried trip to the post office in her cotton house dress where she failed to find a letter from her husband, everything looked awful, including the people of Chambersburg. "Feel 'blue' As if everybody shunned me—as if ashamed to let others know their acquaintance with me. O! If Samuel were only at home so we could go west. I do not feel like dressing in my best to go to P.O. and the long and short—if people that do not wish to recognize me in my calico need not do so at all—I wish I were not quite so sensitive."

She passed her time caring for her daughter and sewing. Recreation included quilting and fashioning ornaments of hair. Through it all her heart was in another place. The diary's dominant theme is her love and anxiety for Samuel. Women North and South shared the misery of waiting and watching, something Confederate soldier's wife Octavia Bryant Stephens captured in a letter to her husband. "I can not help looking for you everytime I hear the dogs bark, and at night when I hear the yard gate open I listen for you to come up the steps, how many times my poor heart beats with hope for nothing."[109]

Octavia, her husband Winston, and their families left a rich body of letters, unusually frank for the time in matters of sex and pregnancy. In addition to all the other burdens "Tivie" had to endure during Winston's service, she worried about upcoming childbirth without his support and under the medical care of a drunken neighborhood doctor. She fantasized about an abortion, telling him she'd heard cottonseed tea was effective, if dangerous. It was also reported to be a form of birth control. "I think you or I had better drink some when my trouble is over this time, don't you?" Winston was indignant. "I don't intend to drink cottonseed and don't want you to. If God sees fit to give us children we will with his help take care of them."

THE LITTLE RECRUIT

UNKNOWN WOMAN in a cotton dress. Although we see many women posing in cotton dresses, every-day calicoes were apparently inappropriate for streetwear. Rachel Cormany was snubbed in Chambersburg, Pennsylvania, for wearing calico to the post office.

A year and a half later Winston was dead, shot by a Union sniper. Tivie's diary reports on a month of tragedies and one new life. "With what a sad, sad heart I begin another journal. On Sunday Feb 28th, dear Mother was taken with a congestive chill. on Friday March 4th, Davis came with the news of the death of my dear dear husband. . . . On Sunday, Mar 6th. . . I gave birth to a dear little baby boy, which although three or four weeks before the time, the Lord still spares to me."

Dorothea and William Lemley in later life.

Civil War Sampler, made by Dorothea Klein Lemley, Sheboygan, Wisconsin, 1861-1865, possibly quilted later, 70" x 93". Collection of Carol R. Smith. While Dorothea's husband William was serving as a Private in the Wisconsin Infantry Volunteers, she stitched the appliqué blocks, seven familiar florals and four flags that are uniquely her own. She appliquéd six red stripes of varying widths on the white ground and reverse appliquéd the rings of thirteen stars. The block at the top, with an eagle perched atop a fruit tree, indicates that Dorothea's mind was on her husband in camp. The tents on either side of the tree reflect, as another Civil War quilter punned, that her "heart was intense." The inscription at the bottom was recently embroidered on top of a fading ink signature by Dorothea's great-granddaughter Carol.

Rachel Cormany was ultimately very lucky. Her husband returned to her. Two of every ten soldiers did not come home, and few Americans escaped without losing a family member. After War's first year, Congress entitled Union widows to draw pensions totaling the monthly pay of their dead husbands. Salaries and pensions ranged from $30 per month for generals to $8 for a private. A year later, war correspondent Noah Brooks noted 15,000 applications for widows' pensions, but "only 1200 have been issued, the rest being under examination or having been rejected." If approved, a widow might receive $144 per year, about one-third of a worker's average annual salary. For women accustomed to poverty in the traditional occupations of teacher, seamstress, or boarding-house keeper, the pension could be managed.[110]

Many widows received supplemental income from fraternal organizations like the Odd Fellows or Modern Woodsmen, dedicated to mutual financial support. A portion of funds raised by soldiers' aid societies such as the Women's Relief Corps of the Grand Army of the Republic also went to supporting widows and orphans. Wives of Confederate soldiers received no official financial support during the War and little afterwards from the crumbling Southern social network.

WAR AND PIECES, machine appliquéd by Karla Carney Menaugh, hand quilted by Ann Thomas, Lawrence, Kansas, 1999, 84" x 84". Karla and I were inspired to adapt old patterns for machine appliqué by Civil War samplers such as Dorothea Lemley's (see page 108). We picked our favorite patriotic Union designs and fashioned our own border.

"Frederick, June 17, 1864

To Abraham Lincoln, President of the United States at Washington—

Dear Sir: I take my pen in hand to ask you about the money coming to me from my husband Daniel Spielman who was a soldier in the second Maryland Regiment in Company C who was killed in a fight with the rebs last fall near Boonsborough, Maryland. I haven't got no pay as was coming to him and none of his bounty money and now Mr. President I am a poor widow woman and have no money and have borrowed all what I lived on last winter and this summer too—Now Mr President I can sew and cook and wash and do any kind of work but can't get none—see if you can't get me a place in one of your hospitals and I will go right to work—but I don't want to leave my little girl so I want to get a place what I can take her too. . . . "

Catherine Spielman.[111]

Martha Green Seward Berry married her first husband, Iowa farmer William Seward, in 1860 when she was 22. Two years later he joined the Michigan Infantry. According to family history, they were so poor that he chose to leave Martha and a four-month-old son at home alone because they needed the private's pay of $8 per month. It is more likely he enlisted to earn the $100 bounty offered to encourage enlistments as the War dragged on.

In May of 1864, William was wounded at Spottsylvania, Virginia, reported missing in action, and presumed dead. Martha's despair lifted when she received a letter from him saying he had been captured and shipped to Andersonville, the Confederate prison. The letters ceased in September, renewing her worst fears, which were confirmed after the War when she discovered William had starved to death in prison. A fellow-prisoner had escaped but William was too weak to try. William's friend later delivered his last note. The execution of Andersonville's commander, one of few Civil War officers convicted of war crimes, was Northern retribution for the suffering endured by so many like William and Martha.

In 1867, Martha remarried and had seven more children. Remarriage cost her William's $8 monthly widow's pension, but she continued to collect $2 per month for William Jr. By the time this photograph was taken in 1890, 40% of the Federal budget was paid in pensions for Civil War widows, veterans, and dependent children, one more enormous social cost of the Civil War.

THOMAS NAST'S annual Christmas drawings for *Harper's Weekly* idealized the holiday, the family, and the waiting wife.

A UNION VETERAN, his wife, and daughter pose at the end of the century. His ribbons include one from the veterans' organization, the Grand Army of the Republic (G.A.R.), and she wears the cross of the women's auxiliary, the Women's Relief Corps (W.R.C.), with a patriotic ribbon around her neck.

MARTHA GREEN SEWARD BERRY and her youngest child, Lizzie Leona Berry. Photo about 1890, Lorimar, Iowa. Courtesy of Jeananne Wright, Lizzie's great-granddaughter.
It is too easy to read pain into faces caught in quiet repose by the camera's long exposure time, but Martha's Civil War nightmare seems etched in her cheeks and forehead. Although she left no diaries or letters, her life is told through the family's oral tradition and in public records such as her application for her widow's pension.

UNION STAR, hand appliquéd and hand quilted by Jeananne Wright,
Longmont, Colorado, 1999, 74" x 59".
Inspired by her great-great grandmother's story, Jeananne copied a Civil
War quilt in her collection as a tribute to Martha Green Seward Berry.

"THE LETTER" by Winslow Homer for *Harper's Weekly*, 1863.

You'll need a period pen, ink and stationery, and a little lap desk. You might be able to find reproductions of envelopes with patriotic and humorous designs that were distributed to Union soldiers. You can print your own by photocopying an appropriate image and running the old-fashioned envelopes through a photocopy machine.

They used a fine paper, much like our air-mail paper or vellum. Colors were white, ivory, and light blue. The sheets were used horizontally and folded in half like a greeting card. They usually began writing on the first page and continued through the last. Paper was too precious to waste, and they'd often write on and on just to fill up the page. When paper was in very short supply they'd write around the edges of the paper and sometimes would write one line vertically and then cross over their writing horizontally, creating a grid of writing that made one sheet do for two.

TWO HEIRLOOMS endure across generations in America. One is family quilts; the other, family letters. Not everyone was as literate as Rachel and Samuel Cormany or Tivie and Winston Bryant. Rural and poor people of the time had little education and some could barely string a sentence together. At encampments you will find soldiers who would welcome the offer of a dictated letter home.

Learn Spencerian handwriting (we've been using the Palmer method for generations) from an old penmanship book. I found my 1874 edition for $5 at a flea market. At the end of the century Mr. Palmer simplified the old hand which had odd conventions such as substituting a shape that looks to us like an "f" for a double "s." "Prentiss" then looked like "Prentif." Do your flowery best with a fine-point crow-quill pen and lots of flourishes.

Union Cradle Quilt

Union Cradle Quilt, machine appliquéd and hand quilted
by Barbara Brackman,
Lawrence, Kansas, 1999.

To remember Rachel Cormany, you can make a Union Star quilt with a border of Union eagles. I had a full-sized quilt much like this one stolen in 1998 in Arkansas. The blocks in the original were not stars, but rather the lozenge shape we sometimes call Orange Peel, in the green and yellow counterchange coloration. Fortunately, I'd photocopied the border eagles. The fabric and quilting looked post-War, but the design is perfect to represent Rachel's 1863 cradle quilt, so I made mine in wartime reproduction fabrics.

Rachel was poor, living on her soldier's pay, so she might have used the inexpensive apron checks of the time. Any color scheme from red, white, and blue to scraps of brown calico is suitable, but contrast is important. I appliquéd the stars and eagles by machine, knowing Rachel had a sewing machine. In 1864, she spent a week in the country and wrote of taking the machine with her on vacation.

Size: 46" x 46"

Sixteen blocks, 8" x 8" finished

Border, 7" finished

FABRIC REQUIREMENTS

You'll learn that all fabrics are not equal when you are machine appliquéing. The loosely woven checks and stripes I used are a little bit harder to work with than a tighter weave. You want fabric with a good hand—something soft, but not too limp. Of course it's always smart to prewash to get rid of the initial bleeding and the fabric finishes.

LIGHT-COLORED FABRIC: 2 yards for blocks, borders, and binding

DARK-COLORED FABRIC: 2 yards for blocks, borders, and binding

2 spools of cotton machine embroidery thread in colors to closely match the fabric (for machine appliqué) **or** #50 cotton (for hand applique)

BACKING: 3 yards

BATTING: 50" x 50"

CUTTING

- Cut 8 dark squares and 8 light squares 10" x 10" for the block backgrounds. Trim to $8^1/_2$" x $8^1/_2$" after the appliqué is complete.

- Trace and cut 8 light and 8 dark stars adding $^1/_4$" seam allowance, using the template on page 115.

- Cut 2 light and 2 dark lengthwise strips $7^1/_2$" x 52" for the borders.

- Cut 6 light and 6 dark eagles using the template on page 115.

- Cut the backing fabric into two equal lengths. Piece to create backing (page 118).

- Cut 3 light and 3 dark strips $2^1/_4$" x 42" for the binding.

THE QUILT TOP

Appliqué Blocks
1. Appliqué the stars to the squares and the eagles to the borders (pages 116-117). I machine appliquéd this quilt, my first try at using freezer paper and a machine stitch that is virtually invisible.

2. Sew the blocks into rows. Press.

3. Join the rows. Press.

Border
1. Fold the border strips in half to help with the placement of the eagles. Appliqué the eagles to the border strips.

2. Attach the borders to the quilt top. Miter the corners (page 118). Press.

QUILTING

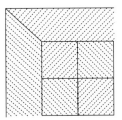

Quilting Design

1. Layer and baste (page 119).

2. Quilt in a 19th-century utility pattern. I used double diagonal lines, changing direction in each block. I quilted across the stars and eagles, ignoring the appliqué. This goes faster than stopping and starting again, and it's what quilters like Rachel Cormany would have done.

3. Bind the quilt (page 119).

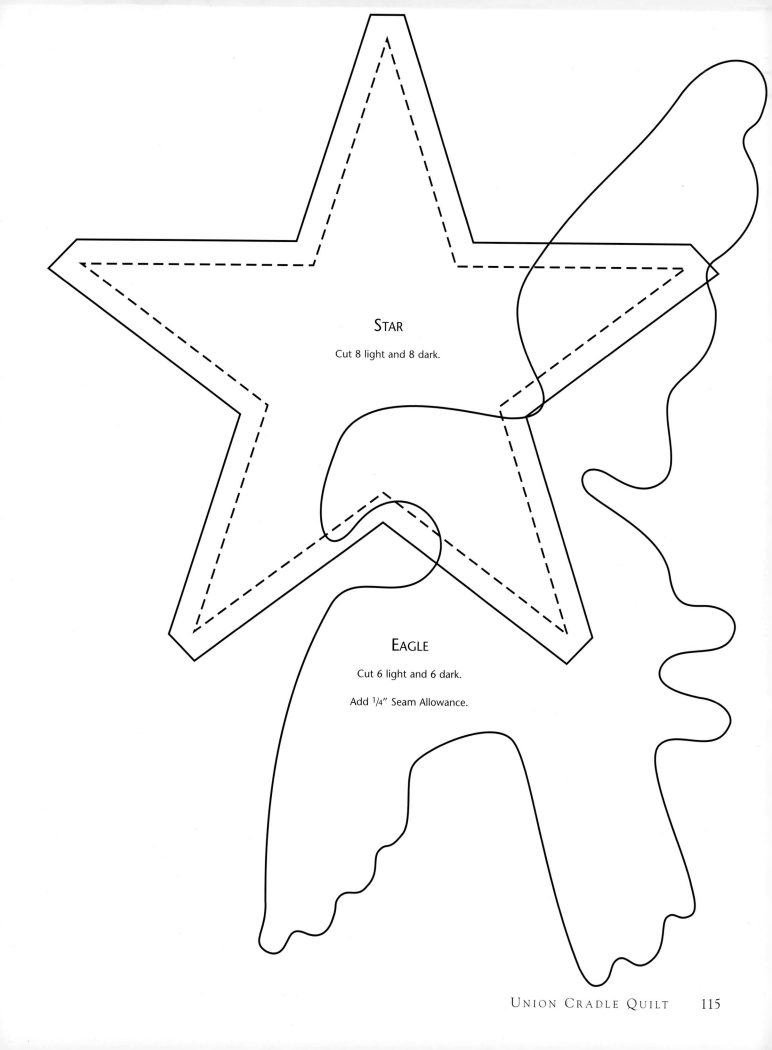

STAR

Cut 8 light and 8 dark.

EAGLE

Cut 6 light and 6 dark.

Add 1/4" Seam Allowance.

APPENDIX

BASIC TECHNIQUES

Seam Allowance
Use standard $1/4$" seam allowance for all stitching.

Hand Appliqué
1. Trace the appliqué shape onto template plastic or paper, then cut out the shape without adding seam allowances.

2. Draw the template shape onto the right side of the appliqué fabric using a fabric marking tool.

3. Cut out the appliqué shape $1/4$" larger than the drawn line.

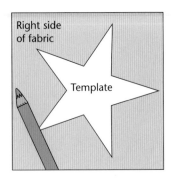

4. Position the shape(s) right-side-up on the right side of the background fabric and baste $3/4$"-1" inside the drawn line.

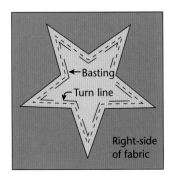

5. Beginning on a straight section of the shape, turn under the seam allowance of a half-inch section to the drawn line, just enough to completely hid the line in the seam allowance.

6. Bring the needle up through the fold (catching only a few threads of the fabric), leaving the knot hidden under the folded edge.

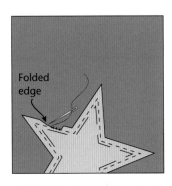

7. Clip the seam allowances as needed to form smooth curves and corners. For sharp points, fold the seam allowance under at the tip (trim slightly if necessary), then fold in first one side, then the other.

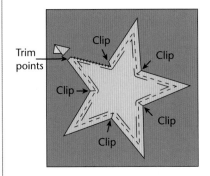

8. Use a blind hem stitch with the stitches very close together, folding under the seam allowance as you go.

9. After appliqué is complete, remove basting stitches.

Reverse Appliqué
1. Trace the shape to be reverse appliquéd on the top fabric, which will become the background shape.

2. Pin this traced fabric on top of the fabric that will become the reverse appliquéd shape.

3. Start cutting away the top fabric $1/8$" inside the traced line to create the $1/8$" seam allowance. Clip into any corners, almost to the drawn line.

4. Fold the seam allowance under and stitch using a blind hem stitch as described above in Hand Appliqué, Steps 6 and 7.

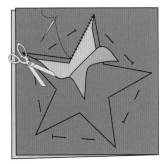

5. Trim and stitch as you go around the shape.

Machine Appliqué

I learned this technique from Cherie Ralston.

To sew this almost invisible stitch you must have a machine that has an adjustable zigzag, which means you can make the zigzag wide or narrow as well as close together or farther apart. You want to adjust your machine to very narrow stitches, very close together.

1. Trace the pattern templates onto the dull side of freezer paper. *Do not add seam allowances. Remember to flip the pattern pieces for the reversible units, or they'll be facing the wrong way.*

2. Cut out the freezer paper shapes carefully on the line.

3. Press the freezer paper (shiny side down) to the *wrong* side of the fabrics. Leave a space between the pieces so you can add a $^1/_4$" seam allowance when you cut them out.

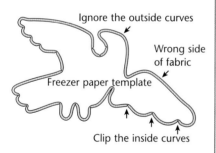

Ignore the outside curves

Wrong side of fabric

Freezer paper template

Clip the inside curves

4. Cut out the paper-backed shapes, adding a $^1/_4$" seam allowance. Clip the inside curves of each piece right down to, but not into, the paper. You don't need to trim outside curves.

5. With a water-soluble glue stick, carefully fold and glue the seam allowance to the dull side of the freezer paper. You can use the point of a seam ripper to manipulate the fabric over the paper as you glue.

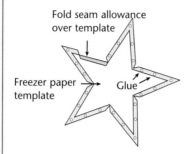

Fold seam allowance over template

Freezer paper template

Glue

6. Position the shapes on the background fabric.

7. One of the keys to successful machine applique is matching the thread to the appliqué shapes that are being stitched. You have to be willing to change thread colors often if you have lots of colors or try to find a good "blender" color that goes well with many shades.

8. Prepare bobbins about half full of machine embroidery cotton for each color you will need. Set your machine for the stitch you choose: overcast, blind hem, or zigzag with a very short stitch length and width. We use the blind hemstitch, which is straight stitches punctuated by a "v" stitch.

9. Stitch the shapes down so most of the stitches run right along the outside of the appliqué shape. You want the occasional tacking stitch to go into the appliqué shape. The hardest part is making sure each tack stitch goes into the applique.

10. When you finish the block you need to remove the paper. Turn the block over and, with small, sharp scissors, carefully cut the backing fabric away, leaving about a half-inch of fabric around the seams.

11. Soak your block in warm water for 15 seconds. Pat it dry with a towel, then snap it diagonally to loosen the paper. Don't snap it so hard you break the stitches (this thread is very fine, so it's easy to break it), but give the block a firm snap both ways. The freezer paper should come out in one piece. If you soak it too long, the paper starts to dissolve and is hard to remove. If you don't soak it long enough, the paper won't come unglued. If you have trouble, snap it again.

12. After the paper is removed, dry the block. You can place it in a warm dryer along with two towels. I've been letting mine air dry on a flat surface. Some people iron them dry, but the colors may bleed with a hot iron and wet fabric.

Traditional Template Method for Piecing

1. Lay a piece of template plastic on top of the shape and trace it either with or without seam allowances using a fine-line permanent pen and a ruler.

2. Cut out the template shape and label it.

3. Use the templates to cut out the necessary fabric shapes for your quilt block.

Sawtooth Grid

Use this method to mass produce sawtooth squares.

1. Cut two rectangles of fabric, one light and one dark, large enough to include all of the squares needed.

2. On the wrong side of the light fabric, draw a grid of squares, each $7/8$" larger than the finished size of the square. Connect the corners with diagonal lines as shown.

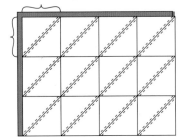

Sawtooth grid finished size + $7/8$"

3. Place the right sides of the dark and light fabrics together. Machine stitch $1/4$" from each side of the diagonal lines. Then cut the horizontal, vertical, and diagonal lines. Press the squares open and you will have sawtooth squares; each square will be half dark and half light.

Border Mitering

1. Attach the four borders to the quilt top, starting and stopping the stitching $1/4$" from the edges of the quilt top.

2. Take the quilt top to the ironing surface and press.

3. Choose one corner and bring the ends of the border out straight, overlapping each other at a 90° angle.

4. Lift the vertical strip and fold it under itself at a 45° angle. Check to be sure the corner is square using a gridded ruler, then press.

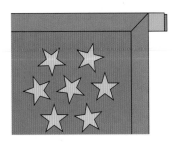

5. Place pins through both border layers near the pressed fold on the wrong side of the fabric. Be careful to keep the corner in position.

6. Fold the quilt top diagonally at the corner, lining it up with the fold on the border corner as shown.

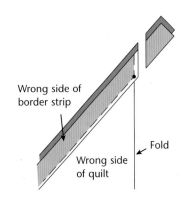

Wrong side of border strip

Fold

Wrong side of quilt

7. Stitch the border corner along the fold line, stopping at the seam allowance stitching.

8. Trim the excess border fabric and press.

9. Repeat for the three remaining corners.

Backing

When the quilt size requires more than one width of fabric for the backing (wider than 42"), it will be necessary to piece it. Trim off the selvages before piecing the backing.

If the backing requires three widths of fabric, stitch the three lengths of fabric together.

If the backing requires two widths of fabric, use one width for the center section. Cut the other width of fabric in half lengthwise and stitch one half to each side of the center section.

Pieced Backing

FINISHING

Layering

1. Place the backing (wrong side up) on a flat surface. Use masking tape to attach the backing to the surface.

2. Position the batting on top and smooth out the wrinkles.

3. Add the quilt top on top of the batting (right side up). Smooth out the wrinkles.

Basting

Baste in a grid approximately 3"-5" apart with long hand stitches.

Quilting

During the 1840-1870 era, quilters used a variety of simple quilting patterns that were utilitarian rather than fancy. They rarely did outline quilting around each piece. We still use some of their utility designs, such as grids or patterns of parallel lines. They were just beginning to use the concentric patterns of curved lines we call fans.

Binding

1. If any of the sides of the quilt are longer than 42", piece the binding strips to create strips that are slightly longer than each side of the quilt.

2. Trim two of the binding strips 1" longer than the width of the top or bottom edge of the quilt.

3. Fold and press it lengthwise.

4. Align the raw edges of the binding strip with the top edge of the quilt, with the extra $1/2$" of binding extending past the corners of the quilt. Stitch the binding strip to the quilt.

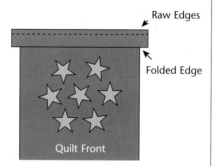

Raw Edges

Folded Edge

Quilt Front

5. Bring the folded edge of the binding to the back of the quilt and slipstitch to the backing. Trim the ends of the binding even with the quilt. Repeat for the binding on the bottom edge of the quilt.

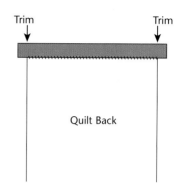

Trim   Trim

Quilt Back

6. Trim the remaining two binding strips $1/2$" longer than the length of the side edges of the quilt.

7. Align the raw edges of the binding strip with one of the side edges of the quilt, folding over the ends of the binding strip by $1/4$". Stitch the binding strip to the quilt.

Quilt Back

To Read More In Their Own Words

Chapter 1

The Lecturer

Loving Warriors: Selected Letters of Lucy Stone & Henry B. Blackwell, 1853-1893. Leslie Wheeler, editor. (New York: Dial Press, 1981). An intimate view of a romance between equals.

Friends and Sisters: Letters between Lucy Stone and Antoinette Brown Blackwell, 1846-1893. Carol Lasser and Marlene Deahl Merrill, editors. (Urbana, Illinois: University of Illinois Press, 1987). Most of the letters are from Nettie, Lucy's sister-in-law, who was a remarkable woman in her own right, an ordained minister.

The Life and Writings of Amelia Bloomer. D. C. Bloomer, editor. (Boston: Arena Publishing Co., 1895) Reprint: (St. Clair Shores, MI: Scholarly Press, 1976). A loving husband's memories of Amelia. To read more of her own words, see her newspaper, *The Lily.*

Chapter 2

The African-American Woman

Susie King Taylor: *Reminiscences of My Life: A Black Woman's Civil War Memoirs* (Boston: Published by the Author, 1902). Reprint as *A Black Woman's Civil War Memoirs*, Patricia W. Romero and Willie Lee Rose, editors. (New York: Markus Wiener, 1988).

The Journals of Charlotte Forten Grimké, Brenda Stevenson, editor. (New York: Oxford University Press, 1988). A daily account by a fairly well-to-do young intellectual.

Chained to the Rock of Adversity. Virginia Meacham Gold, editor. (Athens: University of Georgia Press, 1998). Letters from free black women in Memphis and New Orleans covering the years 1844-1899, plus a short diary by Catherine Geraldine Johnson. Like Charlotte Forten Grimké's book, this gives terrific insight into the parallel lives led by free black women.

Elizabeth Keckley, *Behind the Scenes or Thirty Years a Slave and Four Years in the White House.* Reprint: (New York: Oxford University Press, 1988).

Martha Griffith Browne, *Autobiography of a Female Slave* (J.S. Redfield, 1857). Reprint: (New York: Negro Universities Press, 1969). A detailed memoir.

Beloved Sisters and Loving Friends: Letters From Rebecca Primus of Royal Oak, Maryland, and Addie Brown of Hartford, Connecticut, 1854-1868. Farah Jasmine Griffin, editor. (New York: Knopf, 1999). I haven't read this yet, but it sounds like another long-buried treasure.

The Narrative of Sojourner Truth by Olive Gilbert (Boston: 1850).

Dear Ones at Home: Letters from Contraband Camps. Henry L. Swint, editor. (Nashville: Vanderbilt University Press, 1966).

Voices From Slavery. Norman R. Yetman, editor. (New York: Holt, Rinehart and Winston, 1970). W.P.A. interviews with people from the mid-twentieth century born into slavery.

Slavery Remembered: A Record of Twentieth-Century Slave Narratives. Paul D. Escott, editor. (Chapel Hill: University of North Carolina Press, 1979). More W.P.A. interviews.

Free At Last. Ira Berlin, et al., editors. (New York: The New Press, 1992). Testimony by slaves and ex-slaves from nineteenth-century sources.

Chapter 3

The Newspaper Correspondent

Julia Lovejoy left two bodies of writings, her lifelong diary and her newspaper columns, which took the form of letters to the editors from 1855 to 1864. There is quite a contrast between her writing for the public and her private diary, which includes little politics and much loss, loneliness, and religious searching. Her unpublished diary is in the collection of the Kansas Center for Historical Research. Many of her newspaper dispatches have been republished as "Julia Louisa Lovejoy, Letters from Kansas," in the *Kansas Historical Quarterly* in the following issues: Vol. XI, February, 1942, pp. 29-44, Vol. XV, May and August, 1947.

Larsen, Arthur J., editor. *Crusader and Feminist, Letters of Jane Grey Swisshelm 1858-1865.* (Westport, CT: Hyperion Press, 1976). Swisshelm had little of Lovejoy's sense of storytelling, so her letters are less dramatic. Swisshelm's autobiography is *Half A Century*, published by Jansen, McClure and Co. in 1880.

Chapter 4

The Refugee

Brokenburn: The Journal of Kate Stone 1861-1868. John Q. Anderson, editor. (Baton Rouge: Louisiana State University Press, 1955). The Stones began the war as a planter family in Louisiana and saw the end as refugees in Tyler, Texas. Kate's youthful optimism is evident in her statement that despite the flight to Texas and the death of her brothers, 1864 was the best year of her life.

Reminiscences of the Women of Missouri During the Sixties. (Jefferson City, Missouri Division, United Daughters of the Confederacy: 1913). Reprint:

(Dayton, Ohio: Morningside House, 1988). Missouri's female Confederate sympathizers are not yet well represented in their own words. This book of memoirs, the best on the topic, contains one diary, the "Journal of Mildred Elizabeth Powell," and numerous anecdotes about events told fifty years later.

The Civil War Diary of Sarah Morgan, Charles East, editor. (Athens: University of Georgia Press, 1991). Sarah Morgan was a young, well-to-do woman turned out of her home by Benjamin Butler's Union troops in Louisiana.

CHAPTER 5

THE NURSE

Hannah Ropes, *Six Months in Kansas by A Lady* (Boston: John P. Jewett and Co., 1856). Reprint: (Freeport, NY: Books for Libraries Press, 1972). *Civil War Nurse, The Diary and Letters of Hannah Ropes*, John R. Brumgardt, editor. (Knoxville: University of Tennessee Press, 1980). I love Hannah Ropes's independence and cool competence. Meet her through her Kansas letters, then follow her to the end of her life in a Washington hospital.

Georgeanna Woolsey Bacon and Eliza Woolsey Howland, *Letters of a Family During the War for the Union 1861-1865*. (New Haven, privately printed, about 1899). Jane Stuart Woolsey, *Hospital Days* (New York: 1870). The Woolseys are a well-documented family of nurses from New York City. Their diaries and letters offer a wealth of information about nursing and the minutiae of everyday life, from fairs, quilts, and clothing to New York gossip. See also the chapter on "The Misses Woolsey," in L.P. Brockett, and Mary C. Vaughn, *Woman's Work in the Civil War* (Philadelphia: Zeigler, McCurdy & Co., 1867).

Louisa May Alcott, *Hospital Scenes*. (Boston: James Redpath, 1863); hard to find but included with several other first-person accounts in Harold Elk Straubing's *In Hospital and Camp*. (New York: Stackpole Books, 1993). Louisa's short book about her experiences as a nurse gives another view of the Washington hospital where Hannah Ropes was "the Matron."

South After Gettysburg, Letters of Cornelia Hancock 1863-1868. Henrietta Stratton Jacquette, editor. (New York: Thomas Y. Crowell Co., 1956). Cornelia's diary is defined by her incredible pluck, with matter-of-fact descriptions of a life surrounded by death. She loved being the only woman in a group of men. One could construct a field hospital from her descriptions.

Ada W. Bacot, *A Confederate Nurse: The Diary of Ada W. Bacot, 1860-1863* (University of South Carolina Press, 1994). After losing her husband and her children, Ada became a nurse in Virginia. It's wonderful to watch her depression lift as she begins feeling useful.

Kate Cumming, *Kate: The Journal of a Confederate Nurse*, Richard Barksdale Harwell, editor. (Baton Rouge: Louisiana State University Press, 1959). A descriptive diary of day-to-day hospital life with all the gore.

Sylvia G. L. Dannett, *Noble Women of the North*. (New York: Thomas Yoseloff, 1959). A narrative history of women's war work focusing on nursing, with most of it told in women's own words from diaries, letters, and memoirs; many of them long out of print and hard to find.

CHAPTER 6

THE SPY

A Lost Heroine of the Confederacy: The Diaries and Letters of Belle Edmondson. Loretta and William Galbraith, editors. (Jackson: University Press of Mississippi, 1990). Belle's emotional ups and downs as she carries contraband through Union lines and escapes to the deep South.

"Journal of Mildred Elizabeth Powell," *Reminiscences of the Women of Missouri During the Sixties*. (Jefferson City, Missouri Division, United Daughters of the Confederacy: 1913). Reprint: (Dayton, Ohio: Morningside House, 1988). Lizzie Powell tells well her story about life in St. Louis's Gratiot Prison.

Rose O'Neal Greenhow, *My Imprisonment and the First Year of Abolition Rule at Washington* (London: Richard Bentley, 1863). This book, the words of the most famous of the women spies, is long out of print, but you may still be able to find a copy.

Sarah Emma Edmonds, *Nurse and Spy or Unsexed: The Female Soldier*. (Hartford, 1864). Sarah dressed as a man to fight as a soldier. The federal government believed her story, issuing her a soldier's pension after the war.

CHAPTER 7

THE PLANTER CLASS

Southern women of the planter class are well-represented in print today, due especially to the efforts of several Southern university presses that publish series of these women's words.

The Diary of Dolly Lunt Burge. Christine Jacobson Carter, editor. (Athens: University of Georgia Press, 1997). Unlike many other women whose diaries record disasters and depression, Dolly is remarkably resilient in the face of war and widowhood.

Heritage of Woe: The Civil War Diary of Grace Brown Elmore, 1861-1868. Marli F. Weiner, editor. (Athens: University of Georgia Press, 1997). Grace is young, rich, unmarried and depressed when the war begins. Her introspective diary gives only a fair account of wartime activities until the last years, when she becomes more descriptive.

When the World Ended: The Diary of Emma LeConte, Earl Schenck Miers, editor. (New York: Oxford University Press, 1957). Emma's dramatic tale of the last four months in Columbia focuses on her Confederate patriotism as she laments the enormous changes in her life.

Susan Dabney Smedes, *Memorials of a Southern Planter* (Baltimore: Cushings and Bailey, 1887). Rather than the memoir of her father as the title suggests, this memoir is primarily Susan's recollections of pre-War plantation life near Vicksburg, Mississippi. Her descriptions are valuable, though biased with nostalgia for the "Lost Cause."

Parthenia Antoinette Vardaman Hague, *A Blockaded Family: Life in Southern Alabama During the Civil War.* (Boston: Houghton Mifflin, 1888). Reprint: (Lincoln: University of Nebraska Press, 1991). Parthenia was an unmarried teacher at a plantation near Eufaula, Alabama, during the War. Her memoir is a classic, describing in wonderful detail Southern adaptations to war's deprivations. She's especially good at describing textile production.

The Children of Pride: A True Story of Georgia and the Civil War. Robert Manson Myers, editor. (New Haven: Yale University Press, 1972). A Pulitzer-Prize-winning view of the South through the Jones family's letters to each other.

Diary of Miss Emma Holmes, John F. Marszalek, editor. (Baton Rouge: Louisiana State University, 1979). Emma was a well-to-do Charlestonian who documented her life well.

Mary Chesnut's Civil War. C. Vann Woodward, editor. (New Haven: Yale University Press, 1981). Mary is unusual in her lofty social position, her frankness, and her sense of humor, another Pulitzer-prizewinner.

CHAPTER 8

THE CLERK

A World Turned Upside Down: The Palmers of South Santee, 1818-1881. Louis P. Towles, editor. (Columbia: University of South Carolina Press, 1996). Babe Sims's letters occupy only a few of the 1067 pages in this book of letters and diaries. She's nearly a postscript, but her passionate nature beams through. The material is arranged in chronological order and can become a confusing web of names and relationships. In these large family volumes it's efficient to pick one woman, use the index to find references to her, and read only her letters to get to know the characters one at a time.

The Colton Letters: Civil War Period, 1861-1865. Betsey Coates, editor. (Scottsdale, Arizona: McLane Publications, 1993). Ohio sisters Lina, Nelia, and Delia wrote lively letters among themselves and the rest of the family, detailing Union life during the War.

Sallie Brock Putnam, *Richmond During the War: Four Years of Personal Observation* (New York: C. W. Carleton, 1867). Reprint: (Lincoln: University of Nebraska Press, 1996). Sallie's memoir has much to say about government clerks in Richmond.

CHAPTER 9

THE SOLDIER'S WIFE

The Cormany Diaries: A Northern Family in the Civil War. James C. Mohr, editor. (Pittsburgh: The University of Pittsburgh Press, 1982). Rachel and husband Samuel kept separate diaries while he was in the Army.

Mrs. Hill's Journal: Civil War Reminiscences. Mark M. Krug, editor. (Chicago: Donnelley & Sons: 1980). Sarah Jane Full Hill's memoirs lack the day-to-day detail of the Cormany diaries, but she recalled many details of her life as the Union officer's wife, who was allowed to accompany him on campaigns into Tennessee.

"A Monotony Full of Sadness: The Diary of Nadine Turchin, May, 1863-April, 1864." *Journal of the Illinois State Historical Society*, Volume LXX, #1, February, 1977. Pp. 27-89. The Turchins were Russian émigrés. The wife of a general, she lived with her husband at the front, where she provides an unusual perspective as a foreigner and a woman.

Rose Cottage Chronicles: Civil War Letters of the Bryant-Stephens Families of North Florida. Arch Fredric Blakey, Ann Smith Lainhart and Winston Bryant Stephens, Jr., editors. (Gainesville: University Press of Florida, 1998). A sweet but doomed love story between Octavia and Confederate officer Winston Stephens.

Wartime Washington: The Civil War Letters of Elizabeth Blair Lee, Virginia Jeans Lass, editor. (Urbana: University of Illinois Press, 1991). Lizzie Lee's husband was an officer in the Union Navy. She lived a privileged life as the daughter of Senator Francis Blair and confidante of Mary Lincoln, Jessie Fremont and Varina Davis. She wrote her husband daily during the war, leaving gossipy accounts of Washington politics, her work at the city's orphan asylum and homelife in the country and at Blair House across from the White House.

ENDNOTES

[1] From the *Olive Branch*, quoted in Gerda Lerner's *Grimké Sisters from South Carolina: Pioneers for Woman's Rights and Abolition* (New York: Schocken Books, 1971) pp. 10-11.

[2] Letter from Lucy Stone to Henry Blackwell, Cleveland, Ohio, April 26, 1854, quoted in *Loving Warriors: Selected Letters of Lucy Stone & Henry B. Blackwell, 1853-1893*. Leslie Wheeler, editor. (New York: Dial Press, 1981) pg. 82.

[3] Julia Ward Howe, *Reminiscences, 1819-1899*. (Boston: 1899). Reprint (New York: Negro Universities Press, 1969) pg. 305.

[4] Ibid.

[5] Thomas Wentworth Higginson, *Cheerful Yesterdays*. (Boston: Houghton & Mifflin Co., 1898) pp. 228, 321, 326.

[6] Thomas Wentworth Higginson, *Letters and Journals*. (Boston: Houghton & Mifflin Co. 1921) pg. 59.

[7] Ibid., pg. 60.

[8] Letter from Henry Blackwell to Lucy Stone, Cincinnati, Ohio, September 12, 1855, quoted in *Loving Warriors*, pp. 145-146.

[9] Thomas Wentworth Higginson, *Letters and Journals*, pg. 62.

[10] At the commencement of the War, Dr. Elizabeth Blackwell was an organizer of the Central Relief Association in New York City, which evolved into the U. S. Sanitary Commission.

[11] Letter from S.M. Strickler to S.N. Wood, Junction City, Kansas, April 7, 1867. *Kansas Historical Quarterly*, Volume VIII, Number 2, May, 1939, pg. 211. Lucy Stone's unchangeable maiden name was recalled generations later when a group of New York City's modern women formed the Lucy Stone League in 1921. Their motto: "My name is the symbol of my identity and must not be lost." Ruth Hale and the other Lucy Stoners inspired a new generation of women in the 1970s including this author.

[12] *Chicago Times*, May 21, 1863 quoted in "A Monotony Full of Sadness: The Diary of Nadine Turchin, May, 1863 - April, 1864." *Journal of the Illinois State Historical Society*, Volume LXX, #1, February 1977, pp. 27-89, pg. 39.

[13] Elizabeth Cady Stanton, Susan B. Anthony, Matilda Joslyn Gage, et.al. *History of Women's Suffrage* (Rochester: Susan B. Anthony, 1881-1922).

[14] D. C. Bloomer, *The Life and Writings of Amelia Bloomer*. (Boston: Arena Publishing Co., 1895) Reprint: (St. Clair Shores, MI: Scholarly Press, 1976). The speech is a shortened version and the last two lines are mine.

[15] Letter from Antoinette Brown Blackwell to Lucy Stone, in *Friends and Sisters: Letters between Lucy Stone and Antoinette Brown Blackwell, 1846-1893*, Carol Lasser and Marlene Deahl Merrill, editors. (Urbana, Illinois: University of Illinois Press, 1987) pg. 105.

[16] Letter dictated by Martha. *Letters from Forest Place: A Plantation Family's Correspondence, 1846-1881*. E. Grey Dimond and Herman Hattaway, editors. (Jackson: University Press of Mississippi, 1993) pg. 197-198.

[17] Interview with Martha Colquitt. *Voices From Slavery*, Norman R. Yetman, editor. (New York: Holt, Rinehart and Winston, 1970) pg. 60.

[18] Diary entry by Grace Brown Elmore, *Heritage of Woe: The Civil War Diary of Grace Brown Elmore, 1861-1868*. Marli F. Weiner, editor. (Athens: University of Georgia Press, 1997) pg. 121.

[19] Dictated letters in *Letters from Forest Place*. pg. 198-199.

[20] Interviews with Marriah Hines and Fanny Moore. Yetman, pp. 167, 227. Letter from Mary Jones to Mary Jones Mallard, July 17, 1861. *The Children of Pride: A True Story of Georgia and the Civil War*. Robert Manson Myers, editor. (New Haven: Yale University Press, 1972) pg. 719.

[21] Kate Stone, diary entry. *Brokenburn, The Journal of Kate Stone 1861-1868*. John Q. Anderson, editor. (Baton Rouge: Louisiana State University Press, 1955) pg. 88.

[22] Susie King Taylor, *Reminiscences of My Life: A Black Woman's Civil War Memoirs*. Patricia W. Romero and Willie Lee Rose, editors. (New York: Markus Wiener, 1988) pg. 31. Quotes and biographical information about Susie King Taylor are drawn from her memoir.

[23] Sarah Grimké quoted in Gerda Lerner.

[24] Diary entry by Charlotte Forten Grimké, *The Journals of Charlotte Forten Grimké*, Brenda Stevenson, editor. (New York: Oxford University Press, 1988) pp. 395-396.

[25] Mrs. John A Logan, *Reminiscences of a Soldier's Wife* (New York: Charles Scribner's Sons, 1913) pp. 8-9.

[26] Memoirs of Luvenia Roberts. *Texas Tears and Texas Sunshine*. Jo Ella Powell Exley, editor. (College Station: Texas A & M University Press, 1985) pg. 199.

[27] Letter quoted in Ruth Haslip Roberson, et.al., *North Carolina Quilts* (Chapel Hill: University of North Carolina Press, 1988) pg. 44.

[28] "Hope Harvest." "The Quilting Bee," *Johnson's Lake Shore Home Magazine*, Vol. 3, # 2, February. 1883. pg. 56.

[29] Frances Trollope, *Domestic Manners of the Americans*. (originally published in 1832) Reprint (New York: Alfred A. Knopf, 1949) pg. 420.

[30] "Reminiscences of C. C. Cox," *Texas Historical Association Quarterly*, Volume VI. pp. 127-8.

[31] *The Lowell Offering*, Volume V, 1845, pp. 201-203.

[32] Diary entry by Kate Stone, pg. 88.

[33] John E. Washington, *They Knew Lincoln* (New York: E.P. Dutton & Co., 1942) pg. 89.

[34] "Pens That Made Kansas Free," Kansas Historical Quarterly 6, pg. 376. James Redpath, *The Roving Editor Or Talks With the Slaves in the Southern States*. (New York, self-published, 1859) pg. 300.

[35] Julia Lovejoy, diary entry, March 9, 1831. Manuscript Collection, Kansas Center for Historical Research. Julia's biographical information is from her diary, her published letters, and a biography that Katy Armitage has written for the Kansas Center for Historical Research. Charles Lovejoy was related to famous abolitionists Owen Lovejoy and Elijah Lovejoy, one a congressman and the other a martyr murdered by a pro-slavery mob for his newspaper editorials. Fans of The Simpsons might note that Springfield's minister with the mellifluous voice is named Reverend Lovejoy. Is creator Matt Groening a student of Civil War history?

[36] Miriam Brewster's story is in a clipping called "For a Principle" from an unknown newspaper in a scrapbook at the Kansas Center for Historical Research.

[37] Sara T. D. Robinson, *Kansas: Its Interior & Exterior Life* (Boston: Crosby, Nichols & Co. 1856) pp. 52-53.

38 Julia Lovejoy, a clipping from an unknown newspaper in a scrapbook at the Kansas Center for Historical Research, pg. 251.

39 *The Life and Writings of Amelia Bloomer*. D.C. Bloomer, editor. (Boston: Arena Publishing Co., 1895) Reprint (St. Clair Shores, MI: Scholarly Press, 1976) pg. 45. Amelia Jenks Bloomer (1818-1894) is famous for publicizing reform dress (see Chapter 1), but her real achievement was editing and publishing *The Lily*. She issued the first number in 1849 from home in Seneca Falls, New York.

40 A. C. Hardy, Julia's brother, wrote her obituary, saying she "frequently performed the pulpit service, with much acceptance to the people." Clipping from an unknown newspaper in a scrapbook at the Kansas Center for Historical Research, pp. 233-34. Julia Lovejoy, letter from Lawrence to the Concord, New Hampshire, *Independent Democrat*, September 22, 1856.

41 Julia Lovejoy, letter from Douglas County, Kansas to *Zion's Herald*, August 22, 1863.

42 Ella S. Wells, "Letters of a Kansas Pioneer," *The Kansas Historical Quarterly*, Vol. V, 1936, pg. 397.

43 Permelia A. Hardeman, letter of October 17, 1862, in "Bushwhacker Activity on the Missouri Border," *Missouri Historical Review*.

44 Diary entry, March 18, 1861. *Mary Chesnut's Civil War*. C. Vann Woodward, editor. (New Haven: Yale University Press, 1981) pg. 29.

45 Diary entry April 11, 1862. "Strangers and Pilgrims: The Diary of Margaret Tillotson Kemble Nourse," Edward D. C. Campbell Jr., editor. *Virginia Magazine of History and Biography* Vol. 91, # 4, October 1983, pp. 440-508. pg. 452.

46 Letter from Julia Lovejoy, March 18, 1862.

47 Memoirs of Emma I. H. Carey, in the *Wichita Eagle*, January 29, 1907.

48 Letter from Winston Stephens to Olivia Stephens, March 13, 1862. *Rose Cottage Chronicles: Civil War Letters of the Bryant-Stephens Families of North Florida*, Arch Fredric Blakey, Ann Smith Lainhart and Winston Bryant Stephens Jr., editors. (Gainesville: University Press of Florida, 1998) pg. 106.

49 Diary Entry, November 26, 1864. *The Diary of George Templeton Strong*. Allan Nevins and Milton Halsey Thomas, editors. (New York: MacMillan, 1952) pg. 521.

50 Diary entry December, 1862. *Brokenburn, The Journal of Kate Stone 1861-1868*. John Q. Anderson, editor. (Baton Rouge: Louisiana State University Press, 1955) pg. 161.

51 Ibid. pp.162-4, 339.

52 Diary entry, January 3, 1864. *Kate: The Journal of a Confederate Nurse*, Richard Barksdale Harwell, (Baton Rouge: Louisiana State University Press, 1959) pg. 186.

53 *A Virginia Girl in the Civil War 1861-1865*. Myrta Lockett Avary, editor. (New York: D. Appleton & Co., 1910) pg. 54.

54 "The Misses Woolsey," in L.P. Brockett, and Mary C. Vaughn, *Woman's Work in the Civil War* (Philadelphia: Zeigler, McCurdy & Co., 1867) pg. 339.

55 Much of the biographical information about Hannah Ropes is from John R. Brumgardt's introduction to *Civil War Nurse, The Diary and Letters of Hannah Ropes* (Knoxville: University of Tennessee Press, 1980).

56 Letter from Hannah Ropes, *Six Months in Kansas by A Lady*. (Boston: John P. Jewett and Co., 1856) pg. 62.

57 Diary entry, July 15, 1861. *The Diary of George Templeton Strong*, Allan Nevins and Milton Halsey Thomas, editors. (New York: MacMillan, 1952) Volume 2, pg. 165.

58 Quoted in Sylvia G. L. Dannett, *Noble Women of the North* (New York: Thomas Yoseloff, 1959) pg. 60.

59 Letter from Alice Ropes, January 20, 1863 in Brumgardt. pg. 123.

60 Sarah Jane Full Hill, *Mrs. Hill's Journal: Civil War Reminiscences*. Mark M. Krug, editor. (Chicago: Donnelley & Sons, 1980) pg. 94. Letter from Georgiana Woolsey, 1861, in Dannet, pg. 66. Joel Myerson and Daniel Shealy, *The Selected Letters of Louisa May Alcott* pg. xxiv. Letters from Cornelia Hancock, August 12, 1863, and April, 1864, pp. 83, 126.

61 Quoted in Dannet. pg. 72.

62 Letter from Hannah Ropes, *Civil War Nurse*, pg. 57.

63 Dannett, pg. 198.

64 Sophronia Bucklin, quoted in Dannet. pg. 72; Georgeanna Woolsey, quoted in Dannett, pp. 88-89. Letter from Cornelia Hancock, August 7, 1963, *South After Gettysburg, Letters of Cornelia Hancock 1863-1868*. Henrietta Statton Jacquette, editor (New York: Thomas Y. Crowell Co., 1956) pg. 19.

65 Letter from Cornelia Hancock, August 8, 1863, pg. 21. Letter from Kate Cumming, April 25, 1862. *Kate: The Journal of a Confederate Nurse*, Richard Barksdale Harwell, editor. (Baton Rouge: Louisiana State University Press, 1959) pg. 26. Letter from Louisa May Alcott to James Redpath, September 29, 1863, Myerson, pg. 94.

66 Letter from Cornelia Hancock, May 20, 1863, pp. 104-5. Diary entries by Kate Cumming, August 13, 1863 and March 13, 1865, pp. 128, 265.

67 For more about the Double Tie quilts see Jacqueline Atkins's book *Shared Threads* (New York: Viking Studio Books, 1994) pp. 29-33; and Caroline Cowles Richards's diary, *Village Life In America, 1852-1872* (London: T.F. Unwin, 1912). Reprint: (Williamstown, Massachusetts: Corner House Publishers, 1972.)

68 *Reminiscences of the Women of Missouri During the Sixties*. (Jefferson City: Missouri Division, United Daughters of the Confederacy, 1913). Reprint: (Dayton, Ohio: Morningside House, 1988) pg. 241.

69 Ibid. pg. 246

70 Biographical information on Belle Edmondson is drawn from her diary. *A Lost Heroine of the Confederacy: The Diaries and Letters of Belle Edmondson*. Loretta and William Galbraith, editors. (Jackson: University Press of Mississippi, 1990).

71 Ibid. pg. 260.

72 Ibid. pp. 17-18.

73 Lizzie Powell's biographical information is from her diary. "Journal of Mildred Elizabeth Powell," Mary Stella Hereford Ball, editor. *Reminiscences of the Women of Missouri During the Sixties*. pp. 148-182. Quotes are from pp. 150- 151.

74 Ibid. pp. 172, 177.

75 Ibid. pg. 182.

76 Sara Rice Pryor, *Reminiscences of Peace and War by Mrs. Roger A. Pryor*. (New York: Macmillan Co., 1905) pg. 223 and Kathlyn F. Sullivan's book *Gatherings: America's Quilt Heritage* (Paducah: American Quilters Society, 1995) pg. 146.

77 Mrs. McPhearson's quilt is pictured in the book *Arkansas Quilts* by the Arkansas Quilters Guild (Paducah: American Quilters Society, 1988) pg. 20, and Sullivan pg. 146.

78 Diary entry by Dolly Lunt Burge. *The Diary of Dolly Lunt Burge.* Christine Jacobson Carter, editor. (Athens: University of Georgia Press, 1997) pg. 128.

79 Ibid. pg. 111.

80 Diary entry by Sarah Rousseau Espey quoted in Kym S. Rice and Edward D. C. Campbell, Jr.'s chapter "Voices From the Tempest: Southern Women's Wartime Experiences," in *Woman's War* (Charlottesville: Museum of the Confederacy, 1996) pg. 74.

81 Diary entry by Dolly Lunt Burge, February 16, 1848, pg. 80.

82 Ibid. November 8 1864, pg. 156.

83 Letter from Maria Bryan, *Tokens of Affection: The Letters of a Planter's Daughter in the Old South.* Carol Bleser, editor. (Athens: University of Georgia Press, 1996) pg. 36.

84 Ibid. February 14, 1862, pg. 124.

85 Ibid. June 3, 1863, pg. 128.

86 Susan Dabney Smedes, *Memorials of a Southern Planter* (Baltimore: Cushings and Bailey, 1887) pg. 224.

87 Diary entry by Dolly Lunt Burge, November 18, 1864, pg. 159.

88 Susan Dabney Smedes, pg. 201.

89 Diary entry by Dolly Lunt Burge. July 20, 1865, pg. 147.

90 Susan Dabney Smedes, pg. 201.

91 Thomas Wentworth Higginson, *Army Life in a Black Regiment.* (Boston: Houghton, Mifflin & Co., 1900) pg. 116.

92 Diary entries of Grace Brown Elmore, pp. 78, 80, 93-94.

93 Diary entry of Emma LeConte January 18, 1865. *When the World Ended: The Diary of Emma LeConte,* Earl Schenck Miers, editor. (New York: Oxford University Press, 1957) pp. 12-13.

94 Parthenia Antoinette Vardaman Hague, *A Blockaded Family: Life in Southern Alabama During the Civil War.* (Boston: Houghton Mifflin, 1888.) Reprint: (Lincoln: University of Nebraska Press, 1991) pg. 49.

95 Grace Brown Elmore, pg. 94.

96 Quoted in the Lawrence, Kansas, *Republican.* January 5, 1860, pg. 1.

97 Diary entry of Madaline Edwards. *Madaline: Love and Survival in Antebellum New Orleans.* Dell Upton, editor. (Athens: University of Georgia Press, 1996) pg. 202.

98 Letter from Leora Sims. *A World Turned Upside Down: The Palmers of South Santee, 1818-1881.* Louis P. Towles, editor. (Columbia: University of South Carolina Press, 1996) pg. 388.

99 Babe's letters are included in the Palmer family letters, *A World Turned Upside Down.*

100 John Beauchamp Jones, *A Rebel War Clerk's Diary,* condensed, edited and annotated by Earl Schenck Miers. (New York: Sagamore Press 1958) pg. 355.

101 Sallie Brock Putnam, *Richmond During the War: Four Years of Personal Observation* (New York: C. W. Carleton, 1867). Reprint (Lincoln: University of Nebraska Press, 1996) pg. 415-6.

102 Putnam, pg. 175; diary entry by John B. Jones, September 1, 1864, pg. 174.

103 Letter from Carolina Colton, July 31, 1864. *The Colton Letters: Civil War Period, 1861-1865.* Betsey Coates, editor. (Scottsdale, Arizona: McLane Publications, 1993) pg. 290.

104 Quoted in William George Clugston's, *Rascals in Democracy,* (New York: Richard R. Smith, 1940) pg. 60.

105 Diary entry by Belle Edmondson. *A Lost Heroine of the Confederacy: The Diaries and Letters of Belle Edmondson.* Loretta and William Galbraith, editors. (Jackson: University Press of Mississippi, 1990) pg. 115.

106 For a picture of Varina Davis's quilt, which is in the collection of the Museum of the Confederacy, see page 111 of my *Quilts From the Civil War* (Lafayette, California: C&T Publishing, 1997). The quote is from a letter written when the quilt was donated.

107 Kate Stone, pg. 355.

108 Rachel Cormany, diary entries. *The Cormany Diaries: A Northern Family in the Civil War.* James C. Mohr, editor. (Pittsburgh: The University of Pittsburgh Press, 1982) pg. 287. Biographical information about Rachel is from this book.

109 Letter from Octavia Bryant Stephens to Winston Stephens, February 21,1863. *Rose Cottage Chronicles: Civil War Letters of the Bryant-Stephens Families of North Florida,* Arch Fredric Blakey, Ann Smith Lainhart and Winston Bryant Stephens Jr., editors. (Gainesville: University Press of Florida, 1998) pg. 206.

110 The Civil War death rate is the highest of any American war, with about 630,000 casualties out of the 3,000,000 men who served. In the North, 16% of the soldiers died; in the South, 25%. Information about War statistics and the widows' pensions is from Amy E. Holmes, "Such is the Price We Pay: American Widows and the Civil War Pension System," in Maris A. Vinovskis, *Toward a Social History of the American Civil War: Exploratory Essays* (Cambridge, England: Cambridge University of Press, 1999) pp.4-9.

Noah Brooks's quote is from his dispatches collected in *Mr. Lincoln's Washington,* P J. Staudenraus, editor. (New York: Thomas Yoseloff, 1967) pg. 144.

111 Letter from Catherine Spielman. *Dear Mr. Lincoln: Letters to the President.* Harold Holzer, editor. (Reading, Massachusetts: Addison Wesley, 1993) pg. 107.

INDEX

Quilts

Activities for Re-Enactors

ABOUT THE AUTHOR

Barbara Brackman lives in Lawrence, Kansas, a town that was at the heart of Bleeding Kansas in the years before the Civil War. She is a historian who is immersed in the mid-19th century, curating exhibits for various museums on topics from quiltmaking and the sewing machine to cowboy boots. She was the historical researcher for *Ride with the Devil*, the 1999 Ang Lee film about the Kansas/Missouri border wars. With Terry Clothier Thompson, she designs reproduction cotton fabrics for Moda. She has written numerous books on quiltmaking and history, including *Quilts from the Civil War* with C&T Publishing.

RAVE REVIEWS FROM THE AUTHOR'S FIRST BOOK, QUILTS FROM THE CIVIL WAR

"This is a book to sit with, read, then use to create a few of the nine quilt projects outlined."

—*American Quilt Retailer*

"Diary excerpts provide an intimate glimpse into the realities of women's lives in the North and the South. This historical background sheds light on the nine patterned quilts, enriching your quiltmaking experience. Finding a quilt you want to make won't be difficult, but putting the book down long enough to start sewing will!"

—*Quilting Today*

"The flavor of those times comes alive with fascinating photos and diary excerpts. The faithful reproductions from the author, a quilt historian, connect the past with the present in nine easy-to-follow projects. A perfect gift for the quilter in your life."

—*Country Victorian*

"Quilt history is at its best, as the author encourages us to make a connection to the women of the Civil War and to understand how the war influenced their quiltmaking. These chapters are full of fascinating details of life on both sides of the Mason-Dixon Line."

—*Quilters Newsletter Magazine*

"This colorful publication portrays extraordinary quilt designs dating from the Civil War era. The text describes the projects and patterns, and also includes information about women from the North and South. This book is not only a practical resource, but an important historical sourcebook."

—*Bookwise Bulletin*

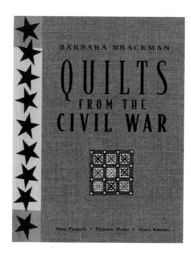

OTHER FINE BOOKS FROM C&T PUBLISHING

For more information write for a free catalog:

C&T Publishing, Inc.
P.O. Box 1456
Lafayette, CA 94549
(800) 284-1114
http://www.ctpub.com
e-mail: ctinfo@ctpub.com

For quilting supplies:
Cotton Patch Mail Order
3405 Hall Lane, Dept. CTB
Lafayette, CA 94549
(800) 835-4418
(925) 283-7883
http://www.quiltusa.com
e-mail: quiltusa@yahoo.com